848.91407 B456w
Benabou, Marcel.
Why I have not written any
 of my books

D1570919

*Why I Have*
*Not Written*
*Any of My*
*Books*

FRENCH MODERNIST LIBRARY

Series Editors:
Mary Ann Caws
Richard Howard
Patricia Terry

MARCEL BÉNABOU

# WHY I HAVE
*Pourquoi je*
# NOT WRITTEN
*n'ai écrit aucun de*
# ANY OF MY
*mes livres*
# BOOKS

RECEIVED

SEP 1 7 1996

Translated by David Kornacker

 

UNIVERSITY OF NEBRASKA PRESS

LINCOLN AND LONDON

848.91407
B456w

Publication of this translation was assisted by
a grant from the French Ministry of Culture. Originally
published in French as *Pourquoi je n'ai écrit aucun de
mes livres*, © Hachette, 1986. Translation © 1996 by David
Kornacker. All rights reserved. Manufactured in
the United States of America. ⊜ The paper in this book meets
the minimum requirements of American National
Standard for Information Sciences – Permanence of Paper for
Printed Library Materials, ANSI Z39.48-1984.

Library of Congress Cataloging in Publication Data
Bénabou, Marcel.
[Pourquoi je n'ai écrit aucun de mes livres. English]
Why I have not written any of my books = Pourquoi je n'ai
écrit aucun de mes livres / Marcel Bénabou;
translated by David Kornacker. p. cm. – (French modernist
library) Includes bibliographical references.
ISBN 0-8032-1239-9 (cloth: alk. paper) I. Kornacker,
David, 1964–. II. Title. III. Series.
PQ2662.E4714P6813 1996 848'.91407-dc20
95-4887 CIP

# CONTENTS

313689

WARREN MOTTE

*Why I Have Not Prefaced Any of Marcel Bénabou's Books*

Marcel Bénabou's *Why I Have Not Written Any of My Books* is one of the most intriguing – and most amusing – books published in France in recent years. It is a *peculiar* book (I use that term in high admiration), full of sudden twists and delightful quirks. The contrary character of its title is amply sustained throughout the book. Bénabou writes against literature in a sense, deliberately balking convention and the expectations of his reader; he proceeds, as Tweedledee might put it, 'contrariwise.' These effects make for refreshing, even astonishing, reading. Yet they also (and here is my caveat lector) make it extremely difficult to account for this book in a preface. For *Why I Have Not Written Any of My Books* is itself prefatory from beginning to end. Or rather, more properly, from beginning to beginning, because wherever one finds oneself in this book, it always seems to be the beginning. On the first page, Bénabou solemnly tells us that the first lines of a book are the most important ones and should be composed with the greatest of care. That which he identifies as his own 'first page,' however, occurs a dozen pages later; and still later there is a new beginning, which must, he says, be a very short sentence. So it goes throughout this book as one advances from threshold to threshold, running ever faster to stay in place.

In his own preface, addressed directly 'To the Reader,' Bénabou lists all the things he will *not* do in his book. He will *not* praise the oral at the expense of the written. He will *not* execrate language, or valorize the inexpressible and silence, or praise life over literature, or argue that inaction is superior to action. He swears up and down that his intent is *not* to destroy literature, and he assures us that in the end doubt and irony will be conquered by seriousness and faith. The contract he offers his reader is thus a contrary one; yet it is nonetheless seductive, promising as it does an appetizing dynamic of struggle, crisis, and ultimate resolution. Bénabou renews that promise in different manners again and again in *Why I Have Not Written Any of My Books*, dangling it in front of his reader's eyes playfully. The ludic quality of that gesture is, I believe, central to his project: Bénabou stages his book as a game in which an author attempts to write an impossible book, impossible because it cannot be merely *a* book but must rather be *the* book, something like the Book of all books. One of the principal rules of the game is that at each turn he must begin again from 'go,' such that every utterance be a prolegomenon, each word a fore-word, in a book that is itself a preface to a far longer, definitive, perfectly embodied – and thus clearly impossible – Book. Genially and with high good humor, Bénabou invites his reader to play this game along with him, pretending that each moment in *Why I Have Not Written Any of My Books* is in fact the inaugural moment of the book.

In that very spirit, allow me to begin my preface again, this time in a more conventional fashion. Marcel Bénabou was born in Meknès, Morocco. According to him, the 'mythology' of his family was a proud one, looking backward over four centuries and including among its notable figures rabbis, cabalists, and miracle workers of various sorts. He mentions that in more recent times his family, though living far from France, entertained a deep interest in French culture, especially French literature, and notes that the writer Pierre Loti described a meeting with one of Bénabou's ancestors in his travel book, *Into Morocco* (1889). Bénabou himself went to study in Paris at the Ecole Normale Supérieure, that hothouse where the most exotic flowers of the French intelligentsia take root. He earned his doctorate in Roman history at the Sorbonne and became a professor at the University of Paris VII, where he continues to teach. Despite what the title of this book suggests, Bénabou is indeed the author of a previous book, and a very learned one at that, *The African Resistance to Romanization* (1976). *Why I Have Not Written Any of My Books* was published in 1986, and it won a distinguished French literary award, the Black Humor Prize. Two books in much the same ironic vein follow upon it, *Throw This Book Away Before It's Too Late* (1992) and *Jacob, Menachem, and Mimoun: A Family Epic* (1995).

In April 1969 Marcel Bénabou joined the Ouvroir de Littérature Potentielle [Workshop of Potential Literature], or 'Oulipo' for short. Founded in 1960 by Raymond Queneau and François Le Lionnais, the Oulipo is a group of writers and mathematicians interested in problems of literary form. That interest is double: on the one hand, they are devoted to the identification and rehabilitation of old, even ancient, forms, such as the triolet or the lipogram; on the other hand, they propose to elaborate new ones, often (but not always) based on mathematical structures. The Oulipo's membership would come to include figures such as Marcel Duchamp, Italo Calvino, Jacques Roubaud, and Harry Matthews. It was Bénabou's longtime friend Georges Perec, the author of *Life: A User's Manual* and *W or The Memory of Childhood*, and in many ways the quintessential Oulipian, who introduced Bénabou to the group. He threw himself into the Oulipo's work with enthusiasm, collaborating with Perec on a project entitled 'Automatic Production of French Literature' (a game much like word golf, but using whole words for pawns, rather than letters), composing 'antonymical' poetry (in which each word in a poem is replaced by its antonym), experimenting with the combinatoric potential of proverbs and aphorisms. During the last twenty-five years, Bénabou has participated assiduously in the Oulipo's public activities as well (readings, colloquia, writers' workshops), and the group has in turn gratified him with the official title Definitively Provisional Secretary.

ix

If I dwell here on the Oulipo, it is because of the tremendous influence it exerted on Bénabou as a writer. That influence can be read, I think, on every page of *Why I Have Not Written Any of My Books*. The ludic spirit that animates the text is largely Oulipian in inspiration, suggesting as it does that playfulness and seriousness of purpose are not mutually exclusive. Like his fellow Oulipians, Bénabou is closely, constantly attentive to form. He plays joyfully on the shape of words, just as he does on the shape of the book, encoding for example names of writers (Edmond Jabès, Perec, and, on a couple of occasions, 'Bénabou') homophonically in his text. A good deal of Bénabou's play is organized mathematically, in fine Oulipian fashion, though the techniques of formal constraint underlying that organization are studiously discreet, verging on the clandestine. The number three recurs insistently in the structure of the text. There are three sections, each containing three further divisions, the first and last paragraphs contain three sentences, and so forth. Bénabou uses three types of discourse: narrative, dialogue, and 'borrowed' language (quotation, allusion, pastiche); each major theme is treated thrice, once in each discursive mode. Appearances notwithstanding, *Why I Have Not Written Any of My Books* is in fact a highly constructed piece of work. Bénabou plays tradition and innovation against each other in a manner that proves their reciprocal complementarity; there is an astonishing literary erudition at work here, all the more surprising in a book that pretends to be unlike any other book. Finally, the notion that the ideal 'Book' exists only as a hypothetical construct in a *potential* state, always waiting to be written, owes at least as much to the Oulipo's theories of potential literature as it does to Mallarmé.

That notion serves as the very motor of *Why I Have Not Written Any of My Books*. It is a source of much of the humor in the text, as Bénabou pursues the Book, chasing it as it flees maddeningly before him. He knows it's out there, he sees it, he has suspected its existence ever since he learned to read, but – damn it all! – he just can't *write* it. His own text at times becomes a meditation on impossibility, as he enumerates, with maniacal attention to detail, the reasons why he cannot write the Book. He argues that one should not attempt to write before one is fully mature. Yet he realizes, with despair, that it is *always* either too early to write – because one's too young, too callow – or too late, because others (Stendhal! Flaubert! Proust! Sartre!) have already constructed such formidable literary monuments. Faced with the classic modernist alternative of writing or living, he finds himself incapable of either, and chooses to adopt a sort of tortured quietism. That choice is amply reflected in the style of *Why I Have Not Written Any of My Books*, for Bénabou's prose is deliberately tortured. His sentences in the original are involuted and laborious; exceptionally long, they strain on the page. David Kornacker has rendered these effects with wonderful fidelity; yet such effects, a source of great fun for Bénabou's reader, must certainly have posed great challenges for his translator.

Bénabou's style, then, illustrates the principal axiom of his book, that writing is torture and, practically speaking, impossible. For Bénabou, at least, if not for others. And there is the rub: why have others succeeded where he encounters only failure and desperation? Those 'others,' both canonical figures and contemporaries, loom ominously throughout the book. Bénabou quotes them or alludes to them continually, comparing his writing to theirs and always coming up short. The first of these intertextual gestures is contained in his title, which plays on Raymond Roussel's *How I Wrote Certain of My Books* (1935). The reference is apt and highly charged with irony, for Roussel's book possesses what is surely one of the most misleading titles in literary history. Purporting to explain such hermetic masterpieces as *Impressions of Africa* and *Locus Solus, How I Wrote Certain of My Books* in fact does nothing of the sort. It is, rather, a reflection on writing itself, on its modes and conditions of possibility. Bénabou suggests that his own title may be read as 'a provocation' and compares his allusion to Roussel to the paradox of the Cretan liar. Taking both provocation and paradox into account, the reference to Roussel in the title helps Bénabou position his book for the reader in two important ways. First, it allows him to declare that his book will not be a conventional one; it is not 'about' anything other than writing. Second, it serves to inscribe the book – both ironically and straightforwardly – under the sign of Roussel himself, perhaps the most exemplary *writer's writer* of French modernism and foremost in a long line of Bénabou's 'others.'

Other 'others' quickly follow. Epigraphs abound in this book, as Bénabou quotes directly from Julien Benda, Novalis, Jorge Luis Borges, Maurice Blanchot, Ecclesiastes, Miguel de Unamuno, Walter Benjamin, E. M. Cioran, Maimonides, Nicholas de Chamfort, Simone de Beauvoir, René Char, Jules Renard, Lichtenberg, 'Mallursset' (a conflation of Mallarmé and Musset), Jean Paulhan, Pierre Reverdy, Jacques Derrida, Pascal, J. Vicens, and Maurice de Guérin. He alludes, explicitly or more obliquely, to Shakespeare (in a rollicking parody of Shylock's speech from act 3 of *The Merchant of Venice*), to Racine, Diderot, Chateaubriand, Hölderlin, Novalis, Stendhal, Poe, Hugo, Flaubert, Henri Amiel, Nietzsche, Rimbaud, Mallarmé, Proust, Gide, Antonin Artaud, Pierre Jean Jouve, Michel Leiris, Sartre, Jabès, and Perec. Other people's writing plays a huge role in the textual economy of *Why I Have Not Written Any of My Books*, and Bénabou muses ironically upon that fact: do those references serve to render his own writing palatable, or is his own writing merely a pretext for these exercises in erudition? Among many other considerations, one appears to be salient: these precursors said 'it' better (or at least said it first). And they are, to a man – *pacet* Beauvoir – writer's writers, just the sort of writer Bénabou aspires to be.

In this vast field of reference, some things stand out. Granted the autodiegetical character of his project, Bénabou compares his book implicitly to certain canonical 'confessional' texts like Stendhal's *Life of Henri Brulard*, Gide's *If It Die*, Leiris's *Manhood*, and Sartre's *Words*, finding these comparisons distinctly unflattering, to say the least. Three figures in particular hover exasperatingly over *Why I Have Not Written Any of My Books*. First Flaubert: if the author of *Madame Bovary* once claimed to 'be' Emma Bovary, so, too, does Bénabou. For he experiences literature like an affliction, from within, so that it becomes his only reality, and an unlivable one at that. His rereading of Flaubert's novel convinces him that his paltry efforts at writing are futile. Bénabou's book is moreover quite patently a *Sentimental Education*, a novel of apprenticeship that mocks that very genre, where irony anticipates irony and the benighted protagonist learns, in effect, nothing. Proust, too, strides mightily through these pages. And inevitably so: how can a writer named 'Marcel' undertake to write about things past without being compared to Proust? And how can this 'Marcel' dare to rival that one? Finally, Bénabou's friend Georges Perec appears frequently in this book. Bénabou plays on Perec's name, refers to him as a 'master,' alludes lovingly to his writings (most notably in a pastiche of the beginning of Perec's first novel, *Things*). Perec's *W or The Memory of Childhood*, like *Sentimental Education*, like *Remembrance of Things Past*, offers a model of writing that Bénabou recognizes as nearly perfect and for that very reason impossible to emulate. If only he, like Borges's Pierre Menard with the *Quixote*, could rewrite those books and call them his own! But of course that won't work either.

Daunted by the writing that surrounds him, Bénabou focuses his haggard gaze on the writing within. Each sentence, each word he writes reminds him that he is, in fact, *writing*; and each sentence in turn shouts that declaration out from the page. *Why I Have Not Written Any of My Books* is a funhouse (to use John Barth's term), a hall of mirrors where the writing subject and the subject of writing are infinitely and comically reflected, to the point of hallucination. The effect of textual specularity, the notion of the book-as-chronicle-of-its-own-elaboration, has been a key feature of contemporary French literature since Gide's *The Counterfeiters* (1925). In recent years, that topos has become in a sense the imposed figure of 'serious' writing, in the absence of which no text can aspire to distinction. In its maturity, then, the topos becomes ripe for parody, and Bénabou plays roundly and gleefully upon the notion of the specular text. Explaining with quite alarming insincerity that his book will not exploit facile 'specular games,' Bénabou intends in fact that his book should *exhaust* the possibilities of writing on writing, exhausting through that same exaggerative gesture the specular text as genre. For never was a book as utterly – and drolly – devoted to itself as *Why I Have Not Written Any of My Books*.

Bénabou also plays on the important (and currently much-vexed) issue of confessional writing, in the same disingenuous spirit. He assures his reader that autobiography and confessional literature in general interest him not one whit. Yet his book is focused squarely on the catastrophic dilemma of *him*-self: though be was 'born to write' (everyone in his circle, family and friends, always quite naturally assumed that he would become a writer), he in fact cannot write. He speaks of how his vocation declared itself during his childhood in Meknès: just as the Jews were the chosen of God, so too he was the chosen of literature. Writing for him was more than a desire; it was an idée fixe. He tells of how he tried to write later in life, during his vacations in the French countryside. Having assembled all his writing utensils, his voluminous notes, his earlier aborted texts, he stares at the empty paper before him: no inspiration comes, and in no vacation spot does he succeed in writing 'his' books. The very *paper* resists him, for God's sake, and this despite the fact that he has erected a veritable cult around it.

He is always buying paper or taking it from others, hoarding it against the day when he'll need it, reams and reams of it. Indeed, Bénabou is an accomplice in the paper's resistance: its white purity awes him, and he does everything to conserve it. In short, as he tries to conquer that which he always thought he legitimately possessed, literature, he is reduced – like Job, like Portnoy – to a long, resounding wail.

In his torment, a new idea occurs to him. Does *not* having written a book perhaps suffice, in itself, to distinguish a man? Despite their ultimate vanity, might his arduous labors make him a hero? The mythological heroes he evokes – Sisyphus, Penelope, Tantalus, the Danaides – are, after all, heroic precisely by virtue of the fact that they labor uselessly, they wait, they yearn, they are beset; and they bear their torment nobly. Such a vision of the heroic fits in nicely with a more contemporary game Bénabou plays, that of 'loser wins,' a familiar gambit of the avant-garde. If the role of the hero as traditionally conceived is unsuitable (too conventional, too confining, or perhaps on the contrary too demanding), perhaps one can be an antihero. Or even a schlemiehl, which is the role Bénabou takes on when he describes himself as an 'irresolute hero, a Hamlet of the library.' The image is an apt one, all the more so in that it points to the real conflict that subtends Bénabou's relations with literature, a conflict between being and doing: though he has always felt that he *is* a writer, what he has always *done* is to read literature rather than write it. He speaks of his readerly bulimia as an apprenticeship; in his mind, he was always reading in order eventually to write. But the writing, alas, never came.

Which brings me to my new beginning and to the only question that makes any sense here: why has Marcel Bénabou not written any of his books? Bénabou poses that question incessantly, addressing his readers directly and immediately, as kindred spirits, assuming that we understand and sympathize with him. And we do, we do! But what are we reading, after all? He tells us twice, echoing Diderot and Magritte and shamelessly indulging his taste for paradox, *ceci n'est pas un livre;* although he admits that it might closely resemble a book, he still maintains that it is a 'nonbook.' But – Hell's bells! – let's get real here. It *is* a book. Hath it not a binding? Hath it not pages, parts, introduction, conclusion? If you spill coffee on it, does it not stain? If you lend it to your brother-in-law, shall he not fail to return it? If you assign it to your undergraduates, shall they not neglect to read the preface?

DAVID KORNACKER

*Translator's Note*

Having little to add to what has been said before me by Warren Motte and to what is to be found following in the body of the book (which I trust will be able to speak for its self-problematizing self), I will limit myself to a few brief remarks.

In several places throughout the novel, the author engages in dialogue with the 'reader.' Obviously, this reader can in fact be masculine or feminine, but the French substantive *lecteur* is masculine, meaning that all pronoun references to that 'reader' are also masculine. I have endeavored to the extent possible to maintain the 'reader's' gender neutrality but have not made special efforts to maintain gender neutrality elsewhere and have specifically identified the author/narrator as masculine.

The translations of the epigraphs throughout the novel are my own from the French in the original except for the E. M. Cioran citations, for which I have used Richard Howard's versions in *The Trouble with Being Born* (New York: Viking Press, 1976).

There are several whom I take this opportunity to thank for their help with this project: Sylvie Weil, for introducing me to Marcel Bénabou and his work; Marcel himself, for his careful reading of my translation and great patience with my queries over the course of two lengthy face-to-face sessions; Warren Motte, for his fine preface and helpful counsel at numerous stages of the translation process; Alan Astro, for his critical reading of a version of the translation and the insights into the original afforded me by his article 'Bénabou bien abouti'; Willis Regier, for charting a smooth editorial course for this translation; and M. Janet Harris, for her intellectual and moral support.

WHY I HAVE NOT WRITTEN ANY OF MY BOOKS

*for Isabelle*

*Understanding that the initial definition of my sub-*
*ject should, while being brief, also be of such rich*
*potential that all the parts of the work would be*
*mere offshoots of it, I spent a long time looking for*
*it; the first sentence of* Belphégor *took me years.*
– Julien Benda, *La jeunesse d'un clerc*

## TO THE READER

First lines of books are always the most important. One cannot be too careful about them. Critics and professional readers shamelessly admit that they judge a work on its first three sentences: if they don't like those sentences, they stop reading right there and, with a sigh of relief, open up the next book.

This is the treacherous cape you have just rounded, reader. Since I will no longer be able to pretend not to notice your presence, please allow me to salute you for your courage, your sense of adventure. On the basis of nothing more than an unfamiliar flag atop cargo whose nature you have no way of knowing, you have thrown yourself into an unknown work – a form of bravery one could well have thought outmoded nowadays.

True – and this is in no way meant to diminish your merit – in this particular case the risks being taken would not seem too terribly great: the work is of modest dimensions, the collection in which it is appearing has been quick to win acclaim, and however little occasion you may have had to acquaint yourself with Oulipian productions, the name printed on the cover might not be unknown to you.

But therein may also lie the danger for you. Who knows into what venture one might be trying to drag you? So let me reassure you on a few fronts and avoid some possible misunderstandings.

You're probably thinking that, however considerable the number of books (all categories included, from the slenderest of satiric pamphlets to the most massive of encyclopædias) that have been produced over the course of the last seven thousand years (an approximation, however rough, must certainly be included in some specialized reference work), it is at the very least unreasonable to claim to base one's distinctiveness on the simple fact of never having taken any personal part in this ever ongoing production; in a word, to your way of thinking, never having written a book should not be enough to define a person, or, for that matter, to dismiss one. Nobody, I believe, would disagree.

And yet, if the sample being considered is narrowed from humanity in all its diversity to a more limited group – for example, the circle of friends, relatives, and acquaintances within which each of us moves and whose judgment we heed – matters appear in another light. In a milieu where writing, and especially publishing books, is not only an activity but a value (at times the only one that remains in the course of an otherwise lengthy decline), one makes oneself singularly conspicuous by staying out of the race. And that singularity merits careful consideration: whether it is found irritating or moving, cause for rejoicing or for embarrassment, it elicits inquiries from friends and colleagues that cannot be ignored.

There are a certain number of ways of responding to such inquiries that I have no intention of using. Here is a rough list of them:

– singing the praises of the oral as opposed to the written;
– railing against language, discrediting the value of words, bemoaning the impossibility-of-any-true-communication;
– ensconcing oneself in the inexpressible, lauding silence as the highest value;
– celebrating life and direct physical contact with reality as superior to writing;
– embellishing upon the themes of abstention-preferable-to-action or of the uselessness-of-doing-anything in a world-destined-for-death-and-destruction-anyway.

If I have not written any of my books, it is certainly not because I dream of writing off literature; I have not opted for sterility as

8

form of accomplishment or for incapacity as mode of production. I do not wish to destroy anything. Quite the contrary, I am determined to respect the laws of the world of books.

Thus, there is an unwritten rule stating that writers, and a fortiori nonwriters, not publish their nonworks. Otherwise publishers, who already don't know what to do with the stacks of manuscripts they receive, would be inundated by a drawer-bottom tidal wave. It is also generally accepted, in all likelihood for the same reasons, that one must be dead (and – at least a little – famous) to have any right to the eventual publication of one's unfinished writings: that jumble of notes, outlines, reflections, and such that any person mixed up with writing cannot help but accumulate throughout the course of a lifetime, a mass of barely polished material waiting to find its place in a future work.

I have no wish to break either of these rules in any way whatsoever. Which does not mean that I am ultimately attempting to construct a model that would explain, in the language of a rigorous determinism, the reasons for which I was not to write.

This book, should it come off, will be the product of a sprint matching various 'demons' (in the Socratic sense, of course). Those of doubt and irony will have given way at the last minute to those of seriousness and faith. But for the moment, I am only a spectator at that race and do not even know for which of the competitors I should be cheering.

THE AUTHOR

9

# TITLE

*The book is the amplified object of the title, or the amplified title. The text of the book begins with the explication of the title, and so forth.* – Novalis

*Why I have not written any of my books.* To many an ear, the phrase will ring like a provocation: would not there be, behind the taking up and refashioning of such a famous title, the presumptuous desire to claim a kinship, indeed (Oh sacrilege!) an identification (at least in manner) with Raymond Roussel? If this were the case, it would be puerile indeed. It was one thing to reveal, half a century ago, in an enigmatic and posthumous text, a few (very few, truth be told) of the secret recipes for producing an œuvre that had had the time to fascinate or intrigue its readers (and what readers!); it is most definitely quite another to lay claim today to the interest of an indifferent public by explaining why books no one has ever heard of (and with good reason) have never seen the light of day.

And the mere substitution of *why* in one title for *how* in the other would be enough, in the eyes of serious people (legion in the world of letters, as everyone knows), to expose the inanity of any attempt at comparing the two.

If it is not a provocation, is it then a paradox, one of those absurd products of the aporia of language, like those sentences that destroy what they state by the simple fact of stating it? (Everyone knows a few by heart, if only the hackneyed example of the Cretan proclaiming all Cretans liars.) In that case, the reader (we have assumed for convenience' sake that there exists at least one) would have every right to cry out (provided, of course, that the reader has a taste for this sort of imaginary dialogue, assuredly a most convenient resource which was once used to a great extent in many a fine novel, then discarded as an oft-used gimmick, but which is now making quite a comeback, thanks to computers, under the melodious name 'interactivity'), so the reader would have every right to cry out in direct address to the author (let us agree to call by that name the one speaking to us) with barely contained indignation, that there is at least one book that he, the author, has written, and that it is precisely this book that the reader himself or herself (that is to say, you) is holding in his or her hands, the very one that is the object of these muddled remarks. To which the author (anyway, that person who is to be presented to us as such henceforth) would have no trouble giving quite a number of replies. Replies that would shut that reader right up. Indeed, everyone knows that if one deigns to give the reader a chance to speak, it is almost invariably only to be able to shine at the reader's expense.

The author could retort that literature is the realm of paradox par excellence. Has not a voice deemed authoritative asserted that the writer is the one within whom *the anguished soul stands beside the levelheaded man, beside the lunatic, a reasonable being and, bound tightly to a mute who has lost use of all words, a rhetorician master of all discourse*? But it is not this line of defense for which the author will opt: other paths of less austere mien are open to him.

He might point out that his title is less paradoxical than it seems. When he declares that he has not written any of his books, he can have meant, depending on which element of his affirmation is emphasized: that he has had his books written by others, a practice which is not rare and from which one does not emerge debased as one once did; that he has written the books of others, a practice at least as common as the preceding one, albeit clearly less well regarded; that he has contented himself with conceiving of his books without going so far as to commit them to paper; or, finally, that he has written something other than what one normally terms a book.

Furthermore, he might add, nothing compels the identifying of he who says *I* with him, the author. Do we even know if he feels the slightest scintilla of solidarity with that character? *I*, after all, is only a word like any other, a simple tool – useful at times – with which it is not forbidden to play, provided, however, that the game does not, as sometimes happens, lead to self-idolatry.

He might admit that for a moment he was tempted, to avoid having to answer for the coming multitude of *me's, myself's,* and *I's* that so worried the author of *Henri Brulard* before him, to invent an Henri Brulard of his own (he would have given him a carefully chosen name such as Marc Gougenheim, Martin Burnacs, or Mathias Flannery) who alone would have borne that responsibility; but he felt himself possessed of neither the disposition nor the stature to rival the realism of census takers – an exercise others have already carried out with too much talent for one to dare have at it. That, he will say, is why he wondered if it was not best to return to the most tried and true of approaches – personal papers entrusted to him in strictest confidence by an unknown stranger. In that case the narrator would have done nothing more than transcribe the confession of this mysterious personage, adding a few comments of his own devising under the half-amused, half-moved eye of an Olympian author. That little stream of doubles between which he would have carefully slipped subtle dissonances would surely have been the safest way to avoid being implicated in all that is to follow.

But his natural indecision would not allow him to take the plunge. Ultimately it struck him as absurd to go to such lengths to defend himself from accusations that perhaps no one was thinking of making. After all, everyone is capable of distinguishing a real author from a potential one, or simpler yet, a writer from his hero.

The reader, if the ponderous subtlety of these preliminaries has not yet caused her or him to lose heart, has in all likelihood already realized that this work does not fully belong to the same category of objects or lie on the same plane as the (nonexistent) books to which the title refers. In other words, to turn a phrase for which everyone knows the extent of the debt owed to Diderot and Magritte, *ceci n'est pas un livre.*

'What's this? Some tardy offspring of the late aliterature, a reincarnation of the now deceased antinovel, a rehashing of the book about nothing?'

'Hey, let's not show our hand too soon, let's leave it to each person to figure out the true nature of what's being presented here and let him or her give it the name that seems most appropriate.'

Oh right, you will say. Our author must really be naive if he thinks he's going to get off with a bit of verbal chicanery as hoary as that. The dialogue begun cannot decently end this way, and any good-faith reader will not fail to ask the question begging to be posed: 'How is this book different from all other books? Is it not made, like them, of words and paper? When it is deciphered, does it not make sense? When it is shredded, does it not make scrap?'

At that point the author will be unable to hide his discomfort However great his esteem for the reader and his desire to please her or him, he will leave that question hanging. For he would obviously be unable to satisfy the reader's curiosity without immediately sawing off the very branch on which he is trying, not without some degree of awkwardness, to sit. Imagine for a moment that he explains why and in what sense this is not a book. Right then and there he takes from the reader all desire to continue.

'Bookstores,' it will be said (the reader is the one speaking), 'are full of books that proclaim their bookishness far and wide and still find no one to read them; what's the use of wasting one's time with a book refusing that designation right off the bat?'

Such reasoning is, of course, irrefutable. Which is why the author will not attempt to refute it. On the contrary, he will admit that he has completely lost his way and run into a dead end. But this chapter is now too far along for him to consider having it change direction. He would therefore prefer leaving it as is and offer another starting from a new basis. To avoid any misunderstanding, he – the author himself – will stay in the background (or at least as far in the background as it is in his power to stay) and will allow his narrator to express himself freely. Let's bet that the reader will get a bit more for his money that way.

## FIRST PAGE

*What tiresome and laborious folly it is to write lengthy tomes, to expound in five hundred pages on an idea that one could easily propound orally in a few minutes. Better is pretending that the books exist already and offering a summary or commentary.* – Jorge Luis Borges

*Those wonderings and works of the mind that attempt the impossible are inexhaustible subjects for meditation. One admires the visible fruits of its art, but one is forever reflecting upon those operations that resulted in nothing visible and whose entire sphere of activity has been in an absence both impenetrable and pure. There the poet has truly grasped the absolute and has hoped to express it in a few words, through a marvel of combinations spirited away from chance.* – Maurice Blanchot

In the beginning, a short sentence. Only half a dozen words; simple words, the first to come along, or almost the first. Assigned above all to mean that here ends a silence. But immediately after, without so much as a paragraph break, there would commence a long sentence in the conditional, one of those old-fashioned periods in which everything would be combined and balanced with care – the choice of the verbs, the logical framework, the number of segments, the length and duration of each one – first to snare then to keep awake the reader's curiosity, to make the reader go step by step (like a child one is taking for a walk down the paths of a garden he is visiting for the first time, like a guest one is taking on a tour of a house he has never entered before) around the entire circle of successive propositions, distributed – in their highly studied diversity – around a single axis, and finally to make the reader stumble, through a maze of interpolations and parenthetical remarks, over a last obstacle (perhaps the least expected at the end of such a journey), a clausula that concludes nothing.

What followed would, of course, maintain this brilliant level. Each sentence would strike the reader. By virtue of its precision. By virtue of its force. And in their rapid succession, together they would form a dazzlingly logical chain.

Yet it would be upon the external appearance of the page that the eye would first glide, then linger, for the play of the white spaces around the letters would give the text an unusual look: the carefully varied, skillfully scattered letters would construct a diaphanous architecture in which emptiness would seem to fill everything. The opaque body of each word would slip discreetly off to one side, as if ready to vanish into the whiteness besieging it. And as one's gaze wandered among the characters, one would forget that these characters make up words, and that those words might have a meaning.

This would be the beginning of a work that would be strong (like a liqueur), and hard (like steel), multiple as well and burgeoning (like everything multiple and burgeoning one can possibly imagine): a nice piece of descriptive prose, one of those pages where there are found together several of the principal qualities extolled by the old masters: syntactical solidity, terminological precision, oratorical power. But above all, what would make this opening sequence precious would be its revealing in the brightest light the true relationship among meaning, images, and sounds, an almost perfect match between the movement outlined by the words and their inner charge. For the time of a page at least, rhetoric would have slipped the bonds of serfdom.

And only at the end of this page, insolent and beautiful as a manifesto, would there make itself heard, coming from who knows where (some place of exile or solitude, no doubt), a voice of imposing sonority. But no listener would be able to reproduce exactly what it had said. And it would be learned, much later, that the voice was dealing with beginning, words, and silence.

Thus (hey, why this thus here already, when it would be more in its place later, in the conclusion of some nice syllogism, for example?), thus, there you have the way I see the first words (well, not really the first ones: before those there will have been a few others, those of the title, the preface – if there is one – and of the epigraphs, dedications, and so on and so forth) of what should be (if I manage to finish it one day, and I know that will not come to pass without difficulty) my first work.

You are surely going to tell me that there are all kinds of works and that you do not see yet to which category this one belongs. A little patience! Why want to be told everything right away? Would your one and only concern be adding one more entry to the list (already quite long, no doubt) of works that you have read and that are carefully arranged by category in your library the way the women were classified by nationality in the catalog of Don Juan's conquests?

Do you really wish that without further delay I draw you into a more or less madcap story, that I present you with more or less well rendered stock characters caught up in more or less plausible conflicts? That will come soon enough, if that is to come. Think instead of the charming compliment that the highly prophetic Mallarmé paid Gide concerning *Paludes*, praising him for having found 'in suspense and secondary issues a form that had to emerge and will be taken up no more.'... So savor the (rare) moment's rest offered you by the present situation. You have already read several pages of this first work by an unknown and still are (at least this is what I dare hope) completely fresh. The subject – if there is one – has not really been deflowered; scarcely have its petals been brushed. Not once to this point has your hand failed to tremble upon turning the page. In short, your expectation is the same as it was at the first line.

## 2

And if I announced to you, for example, that what we have here is a novel whose hero is a writer, an extraordinarily productive writer but stricken with a curse: he knows that the end of his life will coincide with the end of one of his books (but of course he does not know which one). Accordingly, he has imposed upon himself the constraint of never bringing any of his literary projects to term. He throws himself only into inordinately ambitious undertakings, with the hope that, aided by weariness and discouragement, he will be unable to complete them. Each abandoned project maintains his chances of survival: hence, he takes pleasure in multiplying his projects. But dearest to his heart is the one in which he proposes to tell his own story day by day; for he knows that at least that story he will not finish alive.

But the novel could just as easily have another hero in another set of circumstances: it would tell the story of the return to life of a man who, during his youth, without having committed any crime, without having ever been wanted by the law, imposed a heavy sentence upon himself (twenty years of confinement and silence). After conscientiously serving the entire sentence imposed, he finally dares to question this intimate condemnation whose obscure basis from then on he sets about reconstructing.

Perhaps you are among those who do not like allegories, particularly when they strike you as too transparent? So let's just pretend I didn't say a thing and move on to something else. What would you say to a few scenarios of a completely different, more realistic kind? Like this one.

— Let us imagine an old and noble family (in the classical extended sense of the word) coming to the end of a history that has known glorious moments marked by a succession of firm-fisted ancestors. It now lives in a state of nostalgia for this lost past and has pinned on the last of its descendants its hopes for revenge and dreams of restoration. But the recipient of this mission, terrified by the responsibility that has come to fall upon him, a responsibility to which he feels unequal, prefers to take refuge in inactivity.

— Or maybe this one: the story would be that of a man raised to worship books who then, for an indefinite number of years, goes through a crisis, one of the kind that crop up periodically and suddenly lay bare the illusory nature of that which one thought fundamental, a crisis that brings him first to question his values and culture, then at its height takes the form of flight from the persistent temptations of writing, and finally eases, resolving itself into a peace that puts things back in their place. But it is no longer really the same place, and for him everything must be begun anew. This could take the form of a confession: a slow search for what could have been the cause at a given moment for his failures, for what made him stumble.

Readers, I can see your reactions from here: you, good man, you are frowning, and you, dear lady, you do not look amused. None of these stories appeals to you. You see in them only the annoying combination of a few clichés with a like number of commonplaces, a bit of rumpled modernity. What good is it, you will say, to add one more imaginary library to an already overlong series? Don't count on me to contradict you on that score: assertion is not my strong point, and in any conversation, the other person's point of view always seems to me to be clearly superior to my own.

Still, I know how I would have treated each of those subjects. I would have taken pleasure in drowning you in the abundance, the luxuriance, the opulence and profusion of a carefully selected vocabulary, without fearing either excess or plethora, overflow or redundancy. I would have poured out whole litanies of words (by the shovelful, by the cartful, by the wagonful) while paying particular attention to the assonances. For this purpose, I would have scoured one after another twenty specialized dictionaries: the natural history dictionary (ah, the terms from zoology, botany, ornithology, ichthyology…!), medical dictionaries, architectural and musical dictionaries, gastronomical and naval ones. I would have been particularly careful about the appearance of exquisite terms from the domains of hunting, heraldry, and falconry, and of course also those of sailing, still loaded as they are with such poetic nobility. But you would have quickly understood that this ostentation was there only to hide something else: a fundamental worry that, when all was said and done, seemed more honest (and much less time-consuming) to admit without circumlocution. My goodness, it just has been...

3

I am of course a bit late in joining the cohort of those who make the book the subject of their books, who make writing the theme of what they have written. What can I do about it? I am not responsible for the time of my coming into the world. Yes, this theme has, for at least a generation, been the pons asinorum, the doggedly maintained 'tarte à la crème' of a hundred different literary types; yes, I have myself choked on this genre of works and the commentaries they elicit to the point of swearing I would never get in on the act. Yet now nothing else tempts me. But before that, I made a number of attempts by imposing various constraints on myself.

I dreamed of a book in which one would take everything in its simplest, most immediately revealed sense. Nostalgia for literature in a state of nature, still stamped with its innocence, its native purity. For a literature able to restore to me, in its entirety, that feeling of harmony with the world that would envelop me at certain moments of my childhood (on those always sunny Saturday mornings, on the familiar route leading to the synagogue, or the evenings of major holidays, when I would sing the prayers standing to the right of my father). A book whose structure would, in its simplicity, have no inkling of resorting to drawers within drawers; a book from which any kind of mirror would be banished, in which one would search in vain for the least surface able to reflect the image of objects; in short, a book that would allow itself none of the facile effects of *mise en abîme* and specular games.

To manage it, I wanted to limit myself to settings drawn from nature, to elements taken from the heart of the concrete:

26

- the shadow descending one summer evening upon a mountain-lake setting while a small craft moves away from shore with two adolescents on board;
- by the light of a night almost white with the glitter of the moon reflecting off freshly fallen snow, in the background, the red glow of a lantern on an old wooden bridge;
- a linden branch in flower near a spray of poppies in a crystal vase on a heavy table made of rosewood.

But without fail, at the end of a few sentences, I am caught in a sequence of events that I know quite well. Every landscape is transformed into a mood, every setting becomes a symbol.

From every part of them grow mysterious extensions that put them in intimate communication with all kinds of myths. The objects and places to which I try to attach myself seem to dissolve. And I quickly find myself on the edge of the universe of books: the worlds one creates substitute themselves for concrete realities.

Thus, I drafted without too much trouble, and sometimes even with intense jubilation, a great quantity of first pages: were someone to take an interest in them one day, that person could create an anthology that might not be lacking savor. A few times I was also able, with much more effort, to write through to the end a small number of 'first chapters.' But I doubt it would be worth the trouble to gather them: their resemblance would be noticed too quickly. One would always find in them, recognizable in his various disguises, the same indecisive, library Hamlet with the unsteady step, grappling with the same indulgent reader: dragging the reader along in his wake to have the reader see his favorite places (the dusty wings of a theater in which no play would have ever been produced or staged; the icy waiting room of a train station in an outlying area on a line never put in service; in a recently decommissioned navy yard, the almost complete carcass of

27

a trawler that never went out to sea; the neoclassical peristyle of a model slaughterhouse where no animal's blood was ever spilled); intermittently thrusting upon the reader at the turn of an ordinary phrase confidences about the language and childhood, books and silence; finally trying out on the reader the laborious finds of his style in which the sharp points of a bitter humor form a curious couple with snatches of sniveling pedantry.

With all that, I have never succeeded in completing a first book, as if the prospect of putting together chapters that would no longer be mere beginnings, first fruit, harbingers, or decoys, but that would constitute the elements of an organized whole was enough to remove my desire to continue.

But perhaps it is now you, reader, who, buffeted by all these possibilities, tired of the maneuvers that have you stamping with impatience at the threshold of this work, have once and for all lost your desire to know more about it. In that case, too bad. I mean too bad for me: if I have succeeded, in such a small number of pages, in discouraging you from reading me, even while having not yet said almost any of what I wanted to say, it must be that at bottom I am not he who I thought myself to be. For it is true that, much as I have only ever written inconclusive fragments, I have never ceased to take myself for a maker of literature. A curious situation in point of fact. Don't you think it could finally serve as the subject of a real first chapter more satisfying than the ones that have impudently been inflicted upon you to this point?

# RECONSOLIDATION

*Be admonished: of making many books there is no end; and much study is a weariness of the flesh.* – Ecclesiastes

*The reader looking for finished novels does not merit being my reader: that reader is already completed before having read me.* – Miguel de Unamuno

*Every finished work is the death mask of its intuition.* – Walter Benjamin

*Works die: fragments, not having lived, can no more die.* – E. M. Cioran

*The fools are those who say: at me no one ever laughs.* – Miguel de Unamuno

Chateaumoulin, Andé, Mormoiron, Eygalières, Vert, Port-Cros, Dampierre – I could add a few more names to this beginning of an inventory, but what good would it do? It is not indispensable that this inventory be complete. These names are of places where, for some twenty-odd years now, I have taken refuge for part of the summer: country houses large or small, austere or comfortable, all of which my memory today finds to share a family resemblance.

Scarcely has the school year come to an end when a kind of interior ritual falls into place. I leave Paris after having gathered books, files, and notes, and I solemnly make the decision to devote to writing the whole of my time: the long scorching days of Eygalières or Chateaumoulin, the milder afternoons of the little blue salon of the house in Feucherolles, near Dampierre. Solitude then does not weigh upon me.

Every day, for two, three, or four weeks, I sit facing the same landscape: the dry flanks of the Alpilles, the woods of the Vallée de Chevreuse still covered with mist, the barren slopes of Mt. Ventoux, or maybe the single tree in the garden at Vert whose dead trunk has become almost invisible because it is so encircled by the thick, redoubled outpourings of the ivy that has invaded everything. I, who for a long time never thought really to look at nature, I am initiating myself little by little into minute contemplation. I am learning to distinguish the various grays and ochers of the boulders, the many varieties of green. I know how to follow, and even foresee, the shift of the masses of shadow and light according to the moments of the day: here, the sun is going to make a long ribbon of water surge forth between two deserted banks, there a simple stand of poplars, farther away a few old houses separated by gardens, hedges of honeysuckle, jasmine, and clematis. I have forbidden myself every other form of distraction: neither cigarettes, nor alcohol, nor newspapers, nor music enter this austerely furnished room. The ceilings are without moldings; there is no fabric on the walls, not even a crack onto which one's gaze might wander. But if the landscape before my eyes is forever being transformed, the white paper before me changes, so to speak, not.

1

And yet my first act, from the first day, has been to break out my previous writings, those pages that I regularly reread upon summer's return, to the point that for me they have come to be inextricably linked with heat, the taste of peaches, and the smell of melon. They are sheets of various color, age, and dimension. Some – the largest – come from afar. Battered old companions, they are the ones to which I am particularly attached: they bear crossed-out passages, corrections, commentaries, sometimes dates. The others, less laden with nostalgia and regret, have a more austere appearance: tiny rectangles of paper – a quarter the size of regular sheets – covered in a furious hand difficult to make out which are packed into small, gray-pinstriped Bristol-board folders held shut by slightly distended rubber bands.

I have set them all out on my desk, in little piles; but since no desk is ever big enough to hold them all, I have had to commandeer a card table. And, with satisfaction – for I have been awaiting this moment for months – I have begun to examine them, systematically, trying to follow scrupulously the order in which they were filed.

So I have reread all those earlier lines, short waves that broke before their time. I have scrutinized them at length, sure that within their apparent confusion they hold the key to the enigma they present.

But nothing comes. No illumination. On the contrary. It is as if a kind of erosion had occurred, and I find in these texts but a meager fraction of what I thought I had put into them. Through what series of prisms had they passed to reach this degree of insignificance? Where then was the weight of each word, its volume, its flavor?

These memories, these thoughts, even these landscapes that had once seemed worthy of preservation to me had been, in the course of my noting them, stripped of those few details to which in truth they owed their seductive charm. If I had simplified them in this manner, reduced them to their essentials, it was with the illusion that this would put at my disposal material I could shape to my will and whose density I could always restore according to my needs. But when the time came, I discovered that this was hardly the case: faced with these texts, I have no freedom.

It's that they are but the result of a long process of agglutination. The elements contained within them belong to the multiple lines that have intertwined to form my history, and behind the gaps and contradictions stand the silhouettes of the various characters who have grown old within me.

As usual, I made my first assignment finding for these fragments a new classification system, for I have not lost the desire finally to achieve a coherent whole. But the criteria that serve to define my groups were not long in striking me as arbitrary or downright absurd. Chronology? It imposes the mixing of themes that are without any obvious relation. By theme, then? This method does not take into account the demands of the genre to which each fragment is ostensibly destined. As for alphabetical order, it leads to juxtapositions that are really too funny.

Thus, I come up with only unstable compounds always ready to fall apart. And, like those aphasics who are unable to classify skeins of multicolored yarn, I am incessantly starting over: I move the cards from one pile to another, I break up piles to create other ones that satisfy me no more than the ones that came before. It is an interminable tavern puzzle, a form of solitaire whose rules

I would not know how to explain. For how does one get around in this world ruled by the discontinuous, the undone, the incomplete, the partial? Must I force myself to pursue only the insignificant on the pretense that it alone is the site of signification? Impossible it is to close one's eyes to the absurd disproportion between the effort and the result.

So I put off my organizational task, preferring, to save time, to embark upon the phase of the writing itself. It is at that point that I always discover how miserly my language is: words come to me only parsimoniously, my throat labors to articulate them. Certain ones at times end up coming together; I feel them making me itch; they give the appearance of imposing themselves; but they die before having been noted, or perhaps, obstinately refusing to come to light, remain caught in my throat like a fish bone.

Suddenly my hand relaxes for real. I start upon a page, one of those pages I choose to be of the smallest possible dimension to avoid being blinded by too much blank whiteness. I know that my pen must not part even the least little bit from the paper. It must be as one with it. The slightest separation can be fatal. Above all, let nothing be lost...

A few lines, and even in certain cases only a few words, suffice to satisfy my desire for writing, to quench my thirst to continue. The contact of the pen with the sheet of paper now acts like a magic wand in reverse: it dispels the illusion, returns the mind to its void.

A long quarter hour spent rereading the sentence(s) hastily noted and checking the rhythm by meticulous scansion (avoiding most of all the classic line!) convinces me that clearly any additional effort would be superfluous: these lines are self-sufficient and, good or bad, would not suffer being tricked up with a continuation. And for an instant I feel as if discharged of a debt.

Only, however, to come, immediately thereafter, to the firm conviction that with this new step, minuscule though it may be, down the path of writing, I have created new obligations for myself, new duties, that one day will make claims upon me for accomplishments of an altogether more serious nature. This conviction suffices to set into yet more vigorous motion the mechanism of guilty conscience and paralysis.

Thus, as the summer moves along, my demands diminish. I give up on the book of my dreams. No prize jury this fall will have the pleasure of crowning *Ancient Parapets* or *Blind Windows* with its honors. No publisher will be kicking himself for not having taken, for his most prestigious series, *The Schoolboy's Long Ways Round*, or for not having printed over a hundred thousand copies of *Chestnuts in the Fire*. Not one critic writing for a magazine will be able to boast of having penetrated the secret of *Cryptograms* or offered to his readers for their admiration *A Little Something for a Rainy Day*. When booksellers are dressing their windows for the holidays, they won't have *Cartes Blanches*; and the public will not come en masse in search of *Manna*. For all that, I don't take refuge in 'those grapes are sour' thinking, which is not enough to fool me anymore.

So I am ready to content myself with a few pages, indeed with one alone, provided it satisfies me without reservation. Provided above all that it unburdens me, even if but for a short while, of that thought – ever present in the background – that I am yet again in the process of wasting my time. Of wasting it foolishly. Pretentiously.

For in none of these places have I succeeded in writing the books I had planned.

2

I need only find myself obliged to finish an urgent task – having nothing whatsoever to do with my literary preoccupation – for everything apparently to change. This generally begins around midnight when I am on the verge of finishing a scholarly article. Right in the middle of a paragraph, when I think my mind is impregnated enough with its object so that the two thenceforth make but one, when the erudite notes come almost naturally under the pen and I am rejoicing at soon seeing my text finished (for I am a few weeks behind and have already been called to order a bit curtly), a brutal break occurs. A hiatus, then emptiness. But an emptiness that lasts only a flash, just the time needed for me to become aware of it. And immediately thereafter comes an overflowing: sentences step forward, not nebulous and blurry but clean, cutting, ready to be trotted out. Most astonishing of all, they do not fly off, do not turn to dust when I want to pin them down; I can reread them immediately after having copied them down. A great part of what I have written has been written in this manner.

At the rate these illuminations appear, it will no doubt take me a long time to gather the material for even one single book. For my inspired double – this phantom builder of sentences who maliciously impedes my work to dictate his clever discoveries – always comes at those (infrequent) hours of his choosing, drafts (at best) three little pages, then goes away. How to manage to make him give over by the throat and in one fell swoop everything he is holding in reserve? Should I become my own watchman and stay on the lookout for those instants of doubling?

I, who thought myself to be a man of vast projects deftly assembled, am suspicious of these fragments written in a single spurt, as if by bursts. They disturb all the more because, in these intense moments, I do not exercise enough control over what comes to me with regard to somewhat faded elegances and archaic niceties.

Yet I have come to understand that these middle-of-the-night pages are mere safety valves. When complete blockage is at hand – for thought grows exhausted from following simultaneously too many different paths – this overflow itself then gives rise to the words that defuse the tension. But after a few weeks' time, these pages will come to be like so many dead leaves: any trace of sap will have left them. There will remain a withered page.

Thus, these fragments are, from the outset, destined to be consigned to the status of debris. Nothing could establish a place for them in the complex whole to which they are supposed to belong, a whole that will no doubt never exist. Not even on paper.

### 3

Sometimes, however, it seems to me that I am really close to my goal. Works recast twenty times suddenly take shape. At that point the bitter joy that normally seizes me when faced with the certainty of failure fades. I stop losing myself in the labyrinth of my sketches. From one sheet to the next, it is enough for me to change a few words for a link to appear. Directions that seemed contradictory cease to be so.

At those times, by dint of feverish nocturnal euphorias (which can last until dawn, as on that July night in Spéracèdes, when the muffled flutterings of a bat caught in the attic obstinately set the cadence for five hours of intensive work) and cold diurnal manipulations, I would manage to elaborate, thanks to several successive sessions of putting pieces together, a bit more than the germ of a plan: something that was beginning to resemble a text. But what exactly? I have so many projects, and each one is the outcome of a specific necessity ...

I very quickly gave up on writing short stories. My little bits of text would have lent themselves well to that, moreover. Bearers of an image, a smell, a feeling, they are less episodes suited to being inserted into a long story than fleeting fragments of eternity. But searching for these moments of grace stolen from boredom is not my true concern. On the contrary, I would like to call up the backdrops against which those roving remains of memory stand out.

At other moments, when decidedly nothing was coming, it was in turning my back on all my old material that I glimpsed solutions. Yes, ditch the whole jumbled mess there and start from scratch. One day I almost burned everything, seized as I was by the urge to go look elsewhere. Because the fashion was then 'returns' and the portraits of a number of founding fathers were hastily being reburnished, I would have liked to embark upon a return to the healthy delights of the most venerable of forms of literary production: gnomic poetry. I would have created in abundance (at a rate of half a dozen per page at least) austere figures of exotic sages – Celtic bards, learned cabalists, pre-Islamic poets, desert fathers, Irish monks, forgotten masters of Buddhism and Shintoism – whose sole function would have been to proffer, in the instant between their emergence and their disappearance, some obscure or provocative maxim, immediately delivered to the reader without the shadow of a set of instructions. And I too – drawing a most legitimate pride from the barriers that I thus take down – would have built my dwelling: somewhere between Job's barrel and Diogenes' ash heap.

## MOMENTARY PAUSE NUMBER ONE

The reader, whom we shall take the pleasure of thanking for his or her patience, would be within his or her rights to call out to the author here to demand that he explain himself.

'You seemed to have set out,' the reader might tell him, 'with the intention of giving yourself over to an amusing undertaking well suited to entertaining us. And here you go little by little leading us down a completely different path. Eternal beginner, you are now going ahead and confirming the suspicion that hangs over all your ilk: you couldn't write thirty pages without lapsing into confession. And now, of course, you are going to wallow in it shamelessly!'

To which the author would surely reply that to say as much is to misunderstand him badly.

'Not as badly as you might think. Certainly what we have here is not some great revelation of hidden notebooks or the breaking apart of a tough outer shell with a nightmarish crash. We know full well that he will not go on about the shape of his skull or his everyday acts or his thwarted loves. But as for the rest . . .'

'Reader, reader, don't be in a rush to exult. Of course our author's project is still fragile, hardly steadier on its foundations than the dis-jointed fragments of an antique column. But likewise the question he has posed is not simple. It seemed to him that no response was possible without a prefatory turning inward.'

'Ah ha! Navel gazing, navel gazing, I tell you!'

'Yes, but the paths that he has found are various, and he must explore each in turn.'

'Which is to say what? Just how far is he planning on going?'

'As far as he can. But at each new phase of his discovery of himself, he will have to accommodate new fragments of his past.'

'But then are we going to be going around in circles for a long time yet?'

'No doubt. But at that very moment when one thinks the author is going around in circles, he is in fact moving in a spiral. For it is one of his characteristic traits never to consider himself satisfied, to be incapable of stopping, incapable of fixing himself in a posture that he would present as definitive. As for the changing result of his explorations, you are free, reader, to see in it only random reconstructions, belated rationalizations, having no relation with the primeval disorder of things.'

## PROPER USAGE

*Know that fools have written thousands of works and that many people advanced in age but not in knowledge have wasted their time on the study of these books.* – Maimonides

*The writer must be up to speaking about everything in an entertaining and meaningful way, and it is speech and writing themselves that should inspire him while driving him to write and speak.* – Novalis

*There are people who put their books in their library, but M——— puts his library in his books.* – Nicolas de Chamfort

*Most of the books of the current day look as if they were done in a day with books read the day before.* – Nicolas de Chamfort

Don't you go believing, reader, that the books I haven't written are pure nothingness. Quite the contrary (let it be said once and for all), they are as if suspended in the literary universe. They exist in libraries by word, by groups of words, by entire sentences in certain cases. But they are surrounded by so much empty filler and trapped in such an overabundance of printed matter that I myself, truth be told, have not yet succeeded, despite my best efforts, in isolating them and putting them together. Indeed, the world seems to me to be full of plagiarists, which makes of my work a lengthy tracking down, an obstinate search for all those little fragments inexplicably snatched away from my future books.

1

Perhaps you are among those who, like me, can no longer go into a bookstore without feeling a twinge of sorrow, but who don't leave without feeling a certain uneasiness either, indeed a sort of virtual nausea: so many books. And yet for years the main events in my life have been my readings.

True, I have an irrepressible need to read to be able potentially to write, or even simply to be in shape to think. True, my readings almost always influence me: as soon as I have been able to discern in a book the movement that carries it, I take pleasure in inserting myself into it, and I immediately move about in it as in conquered territory. Finally, it is true that the crux of what is original (to my eyes, at least) that I might be able to say would come precisely from that aptitude for being subject to multiple and a priori contradictory influences.

And yet it had all started quite badly. I pompously termed 're-search' the pursuit of a vast and imprecise general learning that would come to complement the mediocre intellectual baggage my studies had left me. But this was in fact nothing more than aimless wandering. Although I invented pressing new needs for myself, because I was dominated less by a taste for knowledge than by a fear of ignorance, I ended up merely jumping in anguish from one subject to the next. Everything was fair game. When today certain pages come to hand, on the occasion of tidying up for example, on which are noted the titles and dates of my readings of those days, I stare at them at length, incredulous and dismayed: what absurd bulimia could have driven me to devour so many works of which I have retained nothing, not even the memory of previously having had them in my hands?

I believed one day to have found the means of putting order in this confused race. It would be enough, bravely identifying myself with my favorite authors, to cover step by step the path they had covered or, put another way, to trace out my readings based exactly on theirs (as their letters, memoirs, and personal diaries revealed them to me). So I set about writing up lists, a task to which I conscientiously and feverishly devoted myself. Then, armed in this way with references, I went out hunting. Paris at the time abounded in used book dealers: the ones along the Seine, of course (among whom I had the thrill of finding a copy – dedicated, in the laborious hand of a beginner filled with respect, to a character named Edouard Caen – from the very first edition of *L'Age d'homme* by Michel Leiris), and in the Latin Quarter, but also those – unknown to me until that time – in the obscure shops in Montparnasse and in the shacks of Clignancourt and Bicêtre.

Old translations of foreign classics would often cause me to stop: miserable, often poorly bound, prewar volumes brought out in forgotten series published by houses that have long since vanished, occasionally accompanied by prefaces with prestigious signatures. One had to buy them without having taken the pleasure of flip-

44

ping through them, for they were always tightly wrapped in a corset of transparent paper there to hide their wear and tear. The heap in my arms would grow and come to be unwieldy. Tired but happy, I would return home. I would carefully arrange my new acquisitions on the carpet and, stretched out on my stomach, would quickly rip off the indiscreet cellophane. Each book would finally open itself up and offer itself to me. For some of them there was no longer even the (ever so delectable) obstacle of pages to be cut. There remained to be accomplished the main thing: immersing myself in reading them. Sometimes that took me weeks; but most often, before having even exhausted my stock, I had already set out hunting again.

This intimate contact with texts sometimes provoked, even in my sleep, a burgeoning of images that I had trouble getting rid of come morning. Thus, at a time when I was taken up solely with the loves of Frédéric Moreau, I approached in my dreams several nights running (which thereafter almost never happened to me again) Madame Arnoux, who had the perfect face of France B. With her I lived two great moments: the first meeting, set by me not on the *Ville-de-Montereau* chuffing full steam ahead down the Seine, but in a discreet and little-traveled alley of the Jardin du Luxembourg (right near the Lycée Montaigne), beneath the blind eyes of a queen of France; then the last meeting, during which she gave me not a lock of her hair but a little gold key, which, she told me with a kiss before slipping away, would make me invisible.

Of course I loved this secret supplement to my diurnal life. All the more so because the traces left me by my scholarly readings – the other side of what I do – were distressingly prosaic. Less linked to the meanderings of my love life, their symbols were distinctly cruder: a scarcely elaborated transposition of my fatigue and anguish at the end of a working day. In one of these dreams (which I give here in its most fully realized form, but certain of whose ele-

45

ments at times found themselves inserted into the weft of other dream sequences), I was caught in the middle of a storm, surrounded by wolves who were devouring, one after another, the trunks of burned trees atop which I was trying to take refuge. The wolves suddenly disappeared and I found myself in the middle of a field of ruins before which I was giving a long harangue. Half hidden behind a column, a poorly made-up character (stunted and sickly in his Roman magistrate's toga) was training on me a rifle with a sight, and I could hear – like a distant, unintelligible murmur – the groans of a crowd gathered behind a barbed-wire enclosure.

All this effort, of course, did not remain without results: in a few years, I had succeeded in giving myself a few scraps of the learning that had been, half a century before, typical of persons of my age. Quite an accomplishment, in point of fact! Even the notes I had forced myself to take (to lend an appearance of toil to what at first had only been passion stemming from the arbitrary whims of the discoveries I chanced to make) came to be unfamiliar to me a few months later.

2

It took me some time to find a parry. The more my intellectual baggage grew, the more, quite naturally, I felt myself capable of refining the questions I might put to books. Little by little, this became a kind of comforting game in which each play could only improve the player's position. From then on, from the all too well constructed network of the lines of each book, I learned to fish, and my modus operandi was akin to those exercises in divination practiced in Rome with the aid of a copy of Virgil. I never set aside a page, a chapter, a volume, before having identified all the elements that seemed in harmony with my own preoccupations (sometimes it was enough to substitute 'I' for 'he' to obtain striking results), and this quest for similarities gave at last the beginnings of a form to certain of my projects.

In this way I nibbled away a portion of the space separating me from writing. Until then, there had been, in my eyes, such a distance between the extreme nobility (which verged at times on a hieratic majesty) of the literary art and the vexing flimsiness of all that I could be led to say that writing could reasonably appear to me only as an unreasonable undertaking; covering that distance would have meant having the effrontery to claim eligibility to join the spare flock of those from whom a public with expectations bordering at times on anxiety awaited something along the lines of a revelation. Now, however, the pleasure of writing was beginning to look to me like another side of the pleasure of reading, and a subtle exchange of tasks was even to be accomplished between these two activities now come to be of a kind.

Thus, in any event, did a new vision of writing establish itself (along with a new way of working): from now on it would only be a question of forcing words, in ever more numerous groups, to enlist in my reveries, to put themselves at the service of my constructions. Henceforth it would be enough for me to mine what was there.

Of course I sought my mother lodes in the area of that literature called personal. But the pleasure I felt from reading the journals, memoirs, and correspondence of great writers was hardly enduring. At first I was reassured to find, among all those who had succeeded in leaving behind a body of work, traces of doubt and dissatisfaction, even moments of real despair, that lent them a brotherly air in my eyes. But upon further reflection, this feeling vanished. 'If even those people suffered so much,' I would say to myself, 'what will it be like for you?' In sum, with my great models I had only two points in common: doubts before writing, uncertainty after. But the in-between remained out of reach.

47

Will I dare bring up in passing the feeling of frustration that certain books left in me? Not because they disappointed me; quite the contrary. But I couldn't keep myself from thinking as I read them that once again I had missed an opportunity. It had, of course, been my place to write this book I had just finished reading: in it I found most of my favorite themes, some of the characters I myself had sketched, even the very twists and turns of what I fancied to be *my* style. And so I felt myself doubly dispossessed: of this real book which could have been mine but which someone else had written, and of the hypothetical book I would have written, a slightly different book (a difference whose lack I felt acutely), if the someone else had not made vain this undertaking.

Amiel was among those who cut off my arms and legs. He had said everything. I could have created a book belonging incontestably to me down to its slightest details (for example, this book here, since after all, Amiel never wrote any of his books either) by combining a few pieces of his *Journal*. I did not do it. I even relegated the *Journal* to a dark corner of my library, behind a heavy row of philology tomes. Out of basic caution, or rather out of reflexive self-defense. For I have only to open one of those wretched volumes to feel myself in a state of perdition: I am sinking into quicksand. I flip pages, reading ten lines here, twenty lines there, and soon I am out of my depth. I try to fight back, but my efforts grow weaker and weaker. Little by little, I surrender myself to a kind of frantic fascination, a resigned torpor, that can permeate whole evenings: only *Madame Bovary* produces a comparable effect in me. And I emerge from it only with travail, soft and limp as a newborn, more convinced than ever of the absolute uselessness of my efforts.

3

I saw only too well where, in the best of cases, all this might well lead. To a book? Certainly not. Rather to a kind of painstaking montage made up of composed pieces and borrowed fragments: insolent pages on which one would no longer really know very well if the citations – some blatant, some discreet – were there to help the ever greater overflow of confidences go down, or the confidences to serve as a framework for a simple exercise in erudition.

## THE SINGLE BOOK

*There is a bad kind of modesty, based on ignorance, that on occasion harms certain superior personages, that holds them back in a kind of mediocrity: which reminds me of the remark made at a lunch to some courtiers by a man of acknowledged merit: 'Ah, sirs! How I regret the time I have wasted learning how much more worthy I am than you!'* – Nicolas de Chamfort

*That is the great advantage of inner life: it grants everyone the privilege of preferring himself to all others.* – Simone de Beauvoir

I long believed that one was born a writer, that it was enough to allow to ripen within oneself for an appropriate number of years this precious seed, and that then one day the first book would appear, as had earlier, at the appointed hour, the first tooth. All this should take care of itself spontaneously and without any particular effort. After the fashion of what happens during certain hours of dreaming, when ideas and phrases suddenly start bursting forth: pages then seem to write themselves, words call forth words, verbs crowd in, adjectives overlap, and in the guise of a bedazzled spectator, one attends a feast prepared by someone else.

It seemed to me that at any moment this feast of writing could come to pass, and that a discreet appeal would be enough to start the machine in motion. Strong in this certainty, I was in no great hurry to start my 'œuvre.' I deliberately declined to risk producing out of impatience one of those youthful, premature, awkward books of which some allow themselves to say that it holds promise or that it is an exercise in style. My wish in those days would have been to be able to publish in one fell swoop and as late as possible something like my complete works: a coherent whole in which would appear, in-their-complex-articulation, the principal-elements-of-my-vision-of-the-world (this was the way one expressed oneself). There I would have explained at my leisure my various positions on the great issues of the time while denouncing, nay castigating, our society for its flaws and laying the foundation for a more-brotherly-and-more-just-society (these themes were absolutely unavoidable in the writings as well as the daily conversation of young people at that time). And even, with a little luck or talent, I might have managed to propose a new kind of hero, to forge a new literary genre, indeed – most ardent wish – a new art form, a revolutionary synthesis (there was the key word) of all that had been known until then.

Accordingly, I left to others the anxieties of a first book and its somewhat crude joys. From the heights of my elevated vantage point, I amused myself contemplating the agitation with which several brilliant youths of my generation were seized. They had decided they would be writers and, with dully utilitarian logic, set out right away to do what was necessary to become writers. Everything suited them: novels, stories, philosophical and political essays. They hurried to bring into the world a first work in perfect resonance with the tastes of the day, as if it were merely a question of completing one more stage in the initiatory journey that had, to that point, comprised the essence of their (our) lives: a stage and a trial conferring the right to enter that society for which I maintained the scorn that was in circulation among my true friends. The refusal to make it, to seize opportunities, to profit from situations; in short, disgust with slickness in all its forms – such were our values still. Any success was suspect, was proof that the one succeeding had not known how to aim high enough. Without an unreachable ideal, there could be no real calling.

So I preferred to wait. On this point as on many others, I conformed as much to my natural bent (that hardly pushes me in general to rush matters or to run ahead of schedule) as to what could be called a feature of my upbringing: in my family, the duty of memory, that is to say the recourse to recollection as a source of renewed life, was accompanied by the privilege accorded to waiting. Waiting conceived of not as a renunciation of action but as an act: an act of complicity with the way of the world. Whence the pleasure I derived from a remark like this one of Buffon's on genius, which 'is but a greater aptitude for patience.' I had adapted it to my

54

own as: not writing is also an act, an action, a deed, sometimes even a good deed.

While I thus stayed in the background, this did not prevent me from lending a hand to a few people (very few, as one can well imagine) whose impatience appeared legitimate to me: less confident about their worth, humble at times to the point of doubting their talent, they urgently needed – it's only human – to prove themselves. And so they set off without further ado on the great adventure, and I thought it my duty to make sure – to the extent my means would allow – that their first works be immediately noticed by everybody and that things turn out successfully for them. I already took real pleasure from this role of behind-the-scenes adviser which I sometimes still play today when the occasion warrants; being ambitious for another, as my dear Amiel puts it, 'is an inoffensive specialty and one where competition need not be feared.' It is true that taking on the part of gray eminence had at least two advantages for me: it allowed me not to be entirely unfamiliar with the intrigues of the small world habitually swarming about literature; at the same time, it confirmed – at very little cost – my belief that my refusal to venture farther into that world indeed resulted from my own free choice. The virginity I insisted on preserving would give yet more solemnity to my future nuptials.

Great, however, was my consternation before those capable of producing works in quantity: the self-dispersion implicit in such behavior was revolting to me, and I could not personally see offering myself up in so many bits and pieces. In my eyes, conceiving of a book as an element in a series was practically akin to imposture. Was this not tantamount to acknowledging the relativity and incomplete nature of one's writings? Could authors worthy of the name thus admit they had not tried to say all? Whereas one must offer only a fully elaborated work, one not linked to a stage in one's life and thought, and only take up the pen to write, if not the very last, at least one of the last possible books. So it was that an obsession with the single book came to be rooted in me. Truth be told, this formulation had been a familiar one ever since my years of learning to read: one of the literature textbooks I liked best, because of the stories in it, was in fact called *The Single Book* (no doubt those who went to French grade school in the late 1940s will recall it). I spontaneously endowed the adjective 'single' with its strongest meaning; indeed, this book appeared to me to be both the only one of its kind and infinitely superior to all others (a logical contradiction that did not trouble me overmuch). I made this vainglorious formulation my own with the secret hope that one day it might well apply to my own (and highly hypothetical) contribution to literature.

I was thrilled to find echoes of these reveries in a few writers whose œuvre I would come upon later. An admission from Pierre Jean Jouve particularly pleased me: 'I have always envied the poet of just one book.' Just one book: you exhaust the lode; neither reserves nor savings nor provisions for the future. Just one book: you undertake a search that knows neither pause nor rest, one that would brook no interruption, not even for the needs of an interim report. For in any event its meaning would only be given at the end.

Gripped by this obsession that endures to this day, I saw any undertaking as premature. What good are books that can by definition be only rough sketches for the one that one wishes to write!

I knew that under these circumstances, I along with my readers, even the most favorably disposed, would always be missing one thing: the possibility of referring back to an earlier work, to juvenilia. Without that, how can one find the cutoff, the sacrosanct break thanks to which, in an orderly career as in a rigorous science, a before and an after can be established? Where is one to situate that reassuring discontinuity that demonstrates in the eyes of the world that the preparatory phase has been completed, that the author has really finished with his classwork, that one can jump into reading the work without fear since one is sure of being in the œuvre proper, not some obscure forerunner or, worse yet, on some unpaved shoulder? I was therefore fully aware of this risk, this lack. But paradoxically, this awareness served only to confirm my refusal to set out.

## 2

*The believer's perdition is meeting his church.* – René Char

And then, I must admit, sometimes there were other alibis. I would tell myself that there were better things to do. That you have to live. Spread your wings. Jubilate and exult. Accumulate joys. Vary your thrills and pleasures. Collect moments of joyfulness and delectation, of happiness and rapture. In other words, tour all the enchantments. I saw the teachings of the masters with which I had stuffed myself converge on just one word: enjoy. *Carpe diem! The roses of life! Sweet little thing, let's go see! The magical study of happiness! Dionysian intoxication! Oh, may my keel break! Live if ye believe! If you think that this that this that this'll go on forever! Happiness and nothing else!* (For it was of course by dint of purely literary references that I exhorted myself not to be snared too soon by the nets of literature.) I would conveniently remember at those moments that I was Mediterranean and that – providing of course that I was able to maintain some distance from 'the vulgar summer of bathers' – I had no need in the end to feel shame at still loving the sea and the sun, sand and salt. And anyway, increasing the breadth of my experience was also to take out a kind of insurance policy, for in this way I was going to have what was required to nourish my work to come. It would not be wagered upon a mere mishmash of childish fantasy; rather, it would be girded by a veritable hoard of good-as-gold lived experience. Create heroes of novels? Of course! But not before having proved my aptitude for being one . . .

Yet at other moments, the thrill of the lived experience faded. 'Petit-bourgeois romanticism,' I was told. Far more noble demands imposed themselves upon me. Transform the world. Be an active participant in history. Defend science from ideology. Words started whirling around inside my head – praxis, masses, theoretical anti-humanism – and I didn't know when their spinning would come to an end.

Theory reigned in those days, and with it a certain terror that slipped into the deepest recesses of our very selves. There is nothing more peculiar than this phenomenon of reigns of theoretical terror, a recurrent one in France which generally crops up in the most protected circles and makes of reality the negligible by-product of a few *concepts*. I had caught the itch, as had many of my closest companions. Truth be told, we were but a short way from the holy of holies. But instead of trying to obtain a place among those few members of the elect to whom it would soon fall to announce the law and establish the dogma of this new, all-conquering Church, I chose to remain in the ranks of the merely faithful. A devout believer, but to the exact extent that this fervor, which normally would have required me to undertake a veritable conversion in my life, on the contrary provided my literary daze with arguments as decisive as they were unexpected.

Certainly writing had, to that point, been more than a desire for me, more than a project, more than a pleasure: it had been a veritable idée fixe. But an idée fixe that, while being practically the only thing on my mind, was not managing to compel that mind to produce. Well, the image of literature that from then on (thanks to the new lights with which I had been illuminated) was imposed upon me – as by turns the ultimate asceticism and the ultimate futility – added doubly to this paralysis.

58

At some moments I saw writing precisely as an austere, exact science that requires a slow, thorough, methodical apprenticeship as well as a long theoretical study before one might be in a position to throw oneself into its practice. But at others, it appeared to me, with an equally evident clarity, that writing was no more than an endeavor for amateurs and idlers cut off from any reality, an activity possessing neither usefulness nor a future and condemned to succumb soon to the weight of its malignant proliferation. Thus, I no longer knew whether what was required was (humbly) to prepare myself to enter-literature-as-one-enters-a-holy-order, there to transpose the rhythm and minutiæ of the gestures of a veritable religious service, or rather to treat literature with joyful arrogance, penetrating it only to deliver the coup de grâce – in short, to move about in it like a moccasin in water.

The uncertainty (and even stupor) into which my mental wanderings in pursuit of the elusive concept of literature plunged me on certain evenings had at least this positive side to them: I never thought for a second of putting myself in question, of acknowledging my own faults, as for example my taste for preparations, preliminaries, and preludes, my spontaneous recourse to abstraction, my mania for analysis (all this no doubt to compensate for my fear of the gravest sin of all: the commonplace). In its unimpeachable objectivity, the verdict of the theoreticians – who sent literature back to its inadequacies and ambiguities – justified my abstention.

Ashamed, however, at times to observe that in these learned matters I was still too often among those who receive more than they give, those who are shaped more than they shape, I ventured to cobble together my own theory. I did so using methods I thought to be exclusively mine. But the result was no clearer. For carried forward at first by a surge of excitement that drew me into the game, I soon found myself abandoned at sea, or rather bound up (as in swaddling clothes) in new ambiguities about which I discovered, after many others who had gone before me, that they were inherent to the use of language. I was particularly stumped by what looked to me like a major obstacle: how literary activity – a debauch (or deceit) immodestly flaunted – can be amusing, indeed downright hilarious (for if you look carefully, what is writing other than drawing two letters and laughing?) on the one hand yet mournful on the other, for, far from acting as a rampart against the fear of death, it can give us only a most macabre reflection of life itself to the extent that, whether it shouts or kicks, whether it rasps or struggles, it is beholden to words, each of which bears death without seeming to.

But it was not only the general problem of language that stopped me; there was also the problem of my own relationship with French, based since childhood on a peculiar mix of superstitious devotion and fervent admiration. I did not fail to ponder the example of Kafka, about whom I had read that he considered himself a 'guest' of the German language. That way of putting it struck a chord: I knew only too well what it meant. If I had to define today my own relationship at that time with the French language, however, that image, with its echoes of intimacy, is not the one upon which I would call; rather, the formulation that would come more spontaneously to mind is 'privileged resident', an expression drawn from the technical vocabulary of government offices. Those who have experienced this situation will understand. It creates obligations that others don't suspect. First and foremost an obligation of gratefulness. To be precise, with regard to French I felt I owed a debt, a debt that could be expunged only by sacrificing the most precious asset I could offer, that is to say a part of my active life. To my mind, it therefore went without saying that I could only become (whatever my profession might happen to be) a sort of servant to the French tongue, a French language worker. But to that first

60

obligation there immediately came to be added the obligation to maintain restraint, something that could be compared to the duty of certain civil servants to remain reserved. On this account, I did not feel myself entitled to touch the majestic edifice to which I had been admitted, yet I rejoiced at having been authorized to tour it indefinitely ... and silently if need be.

I managed all the while to keep from being besotted by the continually repeated arguments trying to dissuade me from fighting battles presented as lost ahead of time, arguments that would have brought me to literary nihilism. Naturally I began to despise the fate that had caused me to be born at a time choked to such an extent with books and writers; I would have liked to have found the way to make plain as day the inanity of so many words, to pour out my resentment upon those who had thought themselves obliged to write them. But that itself was enough, on the days of my greatest scorn, to keep taut the line attaching me in spite of it all to literature.

### 3

*I never feel mature enough for a strong work. Apparently, I am waiting to fall into ruin.* – Jules Renard, 1887

*You aren't mature enough, you say; are you waiting until you start to rot?* – Jules Renard, 1889

Writing nothing before having reached complete maturity thus seemed the primary imperative.

The fear of wasted time did not obsess me yet. On the contrary, it seemed quite fine to sacrifice a few years to a noble cause in this way. I even found that this display of indifference, this serenity conveyed distinction: they left it understood that behind them lurked not doubt but confidence from a kind of pact with the future.

In fact, in my imagination I had already firmly established residence right in the heart of the future and, at the very instant when I was performing the most ordinary of acts (a conversation with a friend in the courtyard of the Ecole on the rue d'Ulm, a lover's stroll on the île Saint-Louis, a lunch on the terrace of some little dive on the rue Mouffetard or the place de la Contrescarpe), I concerned myself first and foremost with imagining what memory I was going to retain later when, after my life had finally found fulfillment in literature, I could recall with nostalgia my former ways and confer upon them the dignity of stages or signs that they would not have failed to attain.

I lived the present like a memory, which exempted me from giving it content. I preferred letting impressions arrange themselves in their disorder, sure that they would not be long in falling into categories of their own accord and that this reordering would be nothing other than the very order of my life made readable.

And so for several years I bore with me in all the worlds with which fate chanced to put me in contact (a fate that still had the good taste to appear in the forms of quite pleasant young women) the classic gaze of indifference or derision that is prompt above all to seize upon signs of inconsistency, sham, and hidden imbalance. But with the hope that one day this gaze would end up becoming a vision.

That lasted a long time, a very long time.

I had saved my strength and built up reserves for tomorrows that were decidedly not coming. What had been a confident wait imperceptibly transformed itself into torpor. From then on, I had the impression that the future was running away from me. Time itself no longer seemed to have any hold on me. Year after year, I found myself identical: same dreaminess, same refusal, same illusions. My face retained its youthful features and I could still easily pass for a quite young man. At times I would rejoice over this lucky suspension of time. It spared me the ordeal of aging, or so I thought. But this taste for the status quo was in fact nothing more than the flip side of a new fear: the fear of seeing that once so eagerly awaited future actually arrive. I had spontaneously adopted and transcribed into my very flesh the technique of those who block the pendulum of their clock to persuade themselves that they are respecting a schedule.

The age of scales and singing exercises had now passed, but the work supposedly ripening in silence was still not on even the distant horizon.

Quite the contrary, literary activity seemed to me at certain (ever more frequent) moments to be a distressingly foolish one. And, as if possessed by the desire to burn bridges and smother possibilities, I put in place one after the other all the mechanisms that would lead to aborting the least project. Works disintegrated the moment they were first glimpsed, disappearing literally without needing to be composed. I would not have been able to say whether it was that reality seemed too banal to merit being transcribed or that words were too flat to render it. But whatever the case, I was only the more obstinate in my defiance and evasion for it.

To this was added the discomfort that my attitude was going to produce among the members of my family. They were growing impatient. Each of them believed himself or herself authorized to criticize my idleness in more or less overt terms. Glory, that glory that they had not stopped counting on for me, was slow in coming. And I, instead of working feverishly to hasten the moment of those triumphs that would also be theirs, gave free rein to my indolence. They had imagined me slaving away to conquer Paris, shining in literary salons, dining night after night with publishers, ministers, and members of the Académie, or at least with the daughters of those fascinating personages, whereas I, thoughtless person that I was, spent my days letting my thoughts wander over old books, writing vague texts that did not fit any particular genre and that I rarely took past the second or third page anyway. I was frustrating their desire for revenge, whose instrument they had unconsciously decided I was to be. For as long as I had needed them, they had done their utmost to make life easy for me. Now, however, they silently reproached me for having developed a taste for that ease. I had thought myself free; I was not: they had claims on me.

Once again, I had to give in to the evidence. Faced with the very classic dichotomy of *writing or living,* which supposes at least the deliberate choice of one path or the other, I responded only by progressively revealing my inaptitude for committing myself to either. Truth be told, I had never taken this choice seriously, for it struck me as mutilating in the extreme. I could not rid myself of the feeling that I was to escape it by virtue of what was essentially multiple in me. Long had I been intoxicated with the abundance and variety of my references, the fruit of an upbringing mixing diverse heritages. I clung to this multiplicity more tightly than to any of my other traits; or rather, in my eyes it included them all. It was neither a fault nor a deviation but the very foundation of my person.

This did not prevent me from spoiling the use I could have made of it, however. For it was linked too closely to my exotic ancestry. And I had not known how to make of my difference the very source of my strength. I should have taken advantage of my distant origins, used geographic happenstance to polish my vision, profited from the lightness given by the voyager's condition; in short, snatched from rootlessness itself the secondary benefits whose bearer it can be. But I did not yet know that one gains the right to be multiple (and other) only if one has shown oneself through a work to be capable of transcending that multiplicity (and that otherness).

64

Thus was produced in my image a reversal whose importance I had not taken in at first blush. Humility gently succeeded pride. The end of my studies had put me up against the wall: I had no 'position,' that is to say I no longer knew where my position was. None of the categories in which one could have enclosed me seemed able to contain me, and I wasn't doing a whole lot to give other definitions of myself.

As a child, at the age when others promise to be Chateaubriand or nothing, I had written that I would be myself or nothing. I had certainly not foreseen that one day I would find myself in the position of being both myself and nothing.

I began telling myself that I was a pretty good embodiment of that absurd character (created, I believe, by Pascal's imagination) who grieved over not having three eyes. What madness drove me not to accept the common lot, not to be satisfied with an eternity of discretion?

But the very choice of silence soothed neither my worries nor my regrets. Certainly, from Rimbaud to Hölderlin and Nietzsche, I was not lacking for models. Nothing dishonorable after all about starting off where those greats had chosen to finish up (perhaps Harar is not only the site of a flight but also the occasion for a veritable redoubling of art). In their hands (if I may put it that way), silence became an arm. It was so heavy, so pregnant with meaning, that it had no more need to hide, to disguise itself in words, as was still the case in quite a number of their poems. But in my hands? I discovered that silence too is difficult to handle. Who knows what (absurd or unflattering) meaning it might be given by those against whom it is used (since it is understood that one always silences oneself – as one kills oneself – against someone)? Under no circumstances did I want it to be possible for someone to believe that I was joining forces – discreetly because ashamedly – with a whole school that, in reality, I abhorred: all those who, pretending to push quietism to its logical limits, safeguard and savor only the ineffable and the subjective, which allows them to slip away with a nonchalant pirouette from the claws of those who would refute them.

A kind of modesty still prevented me from writing out letter for letter words like sterility and failure. Modesty, truth be told, is not the right word. The underlying reason was no doubt once again the resurgence of a family taboo: the refusal to name what one fears. This superstitious fear of the malevolent efficacy of words obliged us to engage in unbelievable oratorical contortions when one had to bring up unfortunate (or merely unpleasant) events and possibilities. Of my misfortunes I spoke only in the third person, attributing them to God only knows what ghost with which, of course, I did not identify myself. Sometimes I preferred to speak of other, less painful things and remembered that on the walls of the catacombs were painted nothing that recalled the horrors of time – no martyrs, no ordeals, no crucifixion – but rather arrangements of fruit and flowers accompanied by doves in flight.

More often than not, however, I chose to be silent.

I had finally understood that life has the annoying habit of not paying in full the obligations it takes on: a rarely solvent debtor, it laughs long and loud at our claims. Happy still are those who can, while awaiting the reckoning by which their account will truly be settled up, pay themselves, at least temporarily, with words.

For me, this meant that from then on I was going to have to set out to conquer that of which I had always believed myself to be the legitimate owner.

# WORD ORDER

*'The French don't want to work anymore, they all want to write,' my concierge told me, unaware that she was then and there passing judgment on all old civilizations.* – E. M. Cioran

*In our day, three smart remarks and a lie make a writer.* – Georg Christoph Lichtenberg

Of all the obscure, or in any event poorly elucidated, facts of my past, the most surprising for me is still this one: why did I come to believe one day that I should write? A simple, seemingly obvious question, yet it took me a long time to feel the need to ask it of myself. It was only after a first long series of aborted attempts that doubt as to the validity of my 'calling' appeared and that I came to wonder about the origins of what, until then, I had considered a kind of determination independent of my will. But after that questioning commenced, it did not cease; indeed, at certain times the better part of my work consisted of responding to it.

The responses I came up with are multiple and at times downright contradictory. One thing is clear, however: the desire to write has aged with me and survived the changing circumstances of my life. Buried in me from birth perhaps, it did not run away with the familiar phantoms of childhood. It knew how to shape itself and adapt to the grievances of an overly docile adolescence. Then, after just barely managing to avoid the risk of being suffocated by year after drawn-out year of study, it could no longer be eradicated, not even by the harsh practice of scholarship. If it is necessary at all costs to swim upstream to the headwaters of this river of words whose periodic floods – although unpredictable and brief – have sustained my daydreams about writing for so many years, it is, of course, along the shores of childhood that one must look. There one finds a curious tangle of causes and effects that even today it is not easy for me to untangle. It is in childhood that I developed my taste for words and the desire to put them together, and it is there as well that I spontaneously took up the themes of my first tries at literature. Thus, childhood provided my writing with its essential motives and motifs. But this double relationship of childhood with writing, which obviously derives from two very separate processes, ended up congealing and making just one magma in my memory. To the point that I no longer know what I owe directly to my childhood experiences and what came to me later, in the wake of attempts I was able to make to recover those experiences and transcribe them.

1

One has never finished with one's childhood. Generally one swings back and forth between a form of bad conscience (is it really worth it for me to lay so much importance on these childish acts?) and a strong dose of worry (am I not neglecting precisely what is most essential?).

The childhoods of others I readily imagine as a blurry scrapbook of memories varying at the whim of moods and moments, a fragile, elusive whole always on the point of dissolving, or even ultimately as a mere sentimental coloring retrospectively projected onto a few beings, objects, and places with no other particular significance. Mine is of another consistency: its traces do not fade and in fact have seemed, with time, to grow more and more deeply embedded while not, for all that, ceasing to be readable on the surface. Is it to a Jewish upbringing, or perhaps to a form of atavism, that I owe this obsession with the past? It indeed seems that there has ever been something of a duty to remember, an obligation to recollect, to make present without cease certain episodes: the covenant with Abraham, the sacrifice of Isaac, the exodus from Egypt, the giving of the Law. And this ancient trait has been further accentuated since the last war by a complementary imperative: the injunction against forgetting.

I certainly had no need of that to fall into the cult of memory: my natural inclination led me straight to it. I am still one of those people who, with their eye firmly fixed on a past reputed to have been happy, enter into life only with reluctance, as if backing into it, when they are not paralyzed outright and nailed to one spot for years. My thoughts, like my passions, I state only in the past (or, if pressed, in the future, provided that this future be very distant): I have a mind (and a heart too) that comes up with the perfect reply after the party is over. Thus, I have lived for a number of years on childhood memories the way others in days gone by lived on the income from their investments. It's true that I had hardly any other resources. But the past comes off in unpredictable patches. And so, like many others, I had the desire to pin it down, to recover it, even recycle it as is done today with old rags and waste water.

To launch me on my way, I had two springboards that had long seemed to me to be worth using: my privileged relations with my entourage, and my no less privileged relations of a completely different kind with the French language.

No one around me, or at least no one in the narrow confines of my family, had ever doubted that my destiny would be a singular one. On what this conviction was based I only asked myself later. I adopted this shared (not to mention flattering) conviction without a second thought and without its seeming any stranger to me than quite a number of other laws, both stated and tacit, governing our family life. It went without saying that the singular destiny that was thus laid out for me was also a glorious one, and that my taste for letters should play the main part.

For among us, relations with language were not some casual thing to be taken for granted. In those relations, the last vigorous, lively vestiges of what had been, in previous generations, the prestige of the family had taken refuge. We had lost our wealth under painful circumstances whose mere mention still evoked, many lustra after the fact, sadness and rancor. But we still retained the intangible privilege of culture, a privilege embodied over the course of nearly four centuries (our family memory had a hard time retracing its roots any farther) by a few remarkable rabbinical figures: one had been a worker of miracles in his distant village of Oufran; another, a daring missionary who went as far as Bukhara soliciting contributions for his pious foundations; and others still were beturbaned cabalists who had chosen to go study and die in the Holy Land. From the memory of certain episodes transmitted religiously from generation to generation, our proud, haughty mythology derived proof of a congenital, hereditary bond with the world of letters along with something like an objective mark of a kind of predestination. A choice place was of course allotted to the long account Pierre Loti gave of the interview he had with my great-grandfather in Meknès in the sumptuous dwelling where our ancestor received him. A curious account, truth be told, for it is a purely exotic decor that is to be found described there with conscientious precision and admiringly minute detail. About the inhabitants of this setting for an oriental tale, however, almost nothing is said. A strange encounter as well – and one about which I have often dreamed – that meeting of the 'Jewish millionaire with the soft face' and the prolific author of *Aziyadé*. Not only because it was the occasion for Loti to incur a debt that he justifiably feared never being able to make good, but also because it symbolically marked for us the new direction of things: French literature and its seductions had penetrated the gilded calm of our family's life.

The elegance and precision of words, the seeking out of picturesque expressions, of precious and even slightly antiquated turns of phrase had all been endowed with the utmost importance. Language was transformed into a veritable talisman: the confusing of a gender led to an engagement's being broken off, the fate of a household was at the mercy of a mistaken agreement or a conjugation error.

In our provincial little colonial society, whose groups were practically airtight and rigidly hierarchical, the cult of letters was, as in the turbulent times of the Roman Empire in decline, what distinguished those who were 'civilized' from everyone else.

Thus there came to me, all but naturally, a kind of passion for culture: culture conceived of as a closed, completed whole which had to be acquired by dint of studies without end (whose merit increased in proportion to their duration) but within which it would have been presumptuous to wish to intervene; culture lived as a model and endowed with part of the prestige that traditional religion was beginning to lose. What drew me was not a certain page, work, or author, which I could find excerpted in the textbooks used by my big brothers, but the whole of what had been able to be written in French. And I saw French literature, of which I still knew almost nothing, as a living being, an organism no element of which one might neglect, or rather as a person never at rest and who existed only through his metamorphoses.

I was still not on familiar terms with France, and the little I knew about the country at times came to me from unexpected sources. For example, I remember having received as a gift on several occasions one of those 'magic penholders' whose sculpted shaft (which I thought was made of ivory) contained the image of a monument. One had only to press one's eye to the little hole in the middle of the shaft to discover . . . the Conciergerie or the palace of Versailles, on a minuscule scale but rendered with perfect clarity. Later, to speak of these monuments and describe the landscapes of France that for me still consisted only of nostalgia, I wanted to find a pen capable of taking the tone appropriate to this type of discovery, a tone of old ivory that from the outset would put the right distance between these things and my gaze, the way, in another context, a pane of protective museum glass would have.

Thus, my relationship with language oriented itself from the outset in a very specific direction. I never ran the risk of confusing things with their name.

73

Most of the words I used were already almost entirely detached from their natural ties to things, and for this reason I found them intoxicatingly light. No heaviness came along to pull them down to the ground. The ones I loved the most (bergamot, nacelle, botargo, galoubet, caillebotis) were attached to nothing I had before my eyes. They were beautiful, shimmering, iridescent bubbles, and their emptiness made them all the more precious to me. What more beautiful toy could one have at one's disposal?

As today, I particularly loved those moments when language appeared to me naked. It was enough for a slightly unusual word to issue from a mouth where I wasn't expecting it to leave me feeling somewhat overwhelmed. The word would immediately disarticulate the discourse that was bearing it, invalidate the logic of the reasoning in progress, and, having created a void around itself, surface alone, filling all the senses with its unusual sonority.

And so I began constructing a kind of fortress, made up only of my favorite words, to which I developed the habit of retiring from time to time. This was not out of indifference to the world or an inordinate taste for solitude; on the contrary, I think I was very well integrated into the little band of schoolboys, made up of neighbors and cousins, to which I belonged. It was just that when it came to the pleasures of language, I had still not found anyone with whom to share them and therefore indulged in my little verbal debaucheries in private. I quickly convinced myself that no reality could equal a happily chosen group of words, and that, I know not why, filled me with true joy, something that no one around me suspected. True, I hardly spoke of it, for all the same I was not sure that this was exactly the kind of thing one admitted freely. To whom would I have dared relate that on certain scorching afternoons, while everyone thought I was taking a siesta, I was in fact undertaking to recopy – line by line and word by word (eliminating as I went only a few expressions that did not strike me as sufficiently 'noble') – a detective story that I had found in the French edition of *Reader's Digest* and that I of course wanted to make say something completely different from what it said? It was the story of a rendezvous missed because of confusion on the part of a young French girl in the reading of a date expressed in numbers by her English lover. Would I have continued to be taken seriously had I confessed then, as I was later to do, that I stockpiled blank white paper?

It is perhaps in this way that there appeared in me a taste for secrets and a habit of doubling that my high-school years would bring out further still. Indeed, entering junior high school marked a kind of rebirth in our world: for the first time, one found oneself flung from the confines of the familial Jewish milieu that until then had constituted our only point of reference. This meant that one had both to conform to the new model being proposed and be careful not to break one's ties with tradition. Quite a tough balancing act, this life on two levels! But it gave the years spent in secondary school the spiciness of a game. A game of double-dealing in which I long took pleasure before growing tired of it.

Having two personalities and two lives coexisting in daily disharmony made up of more or less subtle ruptures came to affect my very way of being. I ended up no longer knowing where or who was the real me.

From then on I mistrusted everything that was double. In me as well as around me. Duality was too close to duplicity. Even the taste for languages, of which I had been so proud since it allowed me still to have at least partial access to what might persist of the old Jewish and Arab culture that for centuries had been the culture of my forefathers and to be at ease everywhere with people of all ages, backgrounds, and social strata, suddenly looked suspicious to me. Beyond the pleasure that the manipulation of at least two languages could bring, I saw a danger lurking: growing accustomed to a form of double language that was much less benign than it had first seemed to me. And I even came to laugh no more at those of my cousins who, although raised as I had been in a certain bilingualism, obstinately refused to speak any way other than in French.

Then, of course, I got myself out of trouble by purely and simply running away. I had elaborated for my personal use a completely new me well above the mediocre incarnations others thought they knew. A me that the vicissitudes of history and colonial geography had maliciously caused to be born too far from its real station in life and its natural place (which must have been some old village in the heart of the Touraine, where the cult of French would have been celebrated daily), like an exotic flower inopportunely transplanted. But the irony of fate had willed that the transplantation have taken place the wrong way around. In reality, I raged at being exotic and lived this exoticism like an unjust exile. And so it was not long before I found I had on my hands the sloughed skins of both a studious high-school student and a Jewish child, two masks with which the arrogant me of the heights did not know what to do.

But childhood does not last forever, and my faith in familial infallibility began to crumble. I sought some basis for what I had been taught and kept on not finding one. I began wondering, not without aggravation, by what path was to come the glory I had been promised. I scrutinized myself, impatient to discover the grain of genius that necessarily had to surge forth one day and astonished that it was so slow to show itself. For nothing decisive came. My successes? They in no way exceeded those one could reasonably expect of the 'gifted, hardworking' pupil my teachers – with a distressing lack of imagination but a reassuring unanimity – encouraged or congratulated from trimester to trimester. To my great shame, I was not even a child prodigy. One day I had to bow to the evidence: the only singular thing I found in myself was that certainty, that obsession with being singular, that was now a very part of me and seemed to have no root other than itself.

Facing it I was in the same strange position as the Jews facing their being the chosen people. Many of the earth's peoples have believed or called themselves 'chosen.' One after another they have created empires and marked mankind's memory with their opulence or their cruelty, something that could at least give their pretensions a semblance of a foundation. The Jews have proceeded in another manner: they have worked at having themselves chosen by pretending to believe – and at times in fact believing (over time, the difference between the two attitudes has ended up fading away) – in the story they themselves have concocted of their having been chosen. So if I wanted to move beyond the impasse in which I found myself, I had to take my situation more seriously. Writing would be the means by which I might be able to give my life the truly singular quality to which I aspired. It would be enough to write the story of what I dreamed of being. True future reality, thus prefigured and in both senses penned in, would not dare not be as I would have previously described it. For I would, of course, have invented only lies overflowing with exactness.

Thus was I relieved of a weight. I no longer needed to look either above me or into the heart of me for the hidden power that would allow me to believe again in the existence of a future: a pen would suffice. But the elegance and convenience of this stratagem hid from me its principal danger: to wit, that in so doing I was imposing upon myself a heavy task that, should some obstacle chance to defer its completion, would not fail – as in the historical example from which I thought myself legitimately able to draw inspiration – to transform the chosen party into a victim.

Everything in this way came to be mixed in my head, and the desire for writing became the great receptacle in which all knots were to be untied and all obstacles dissolved. But there are so many ways to sign oneself over to writing!

## 3

*One hesitates to make cones for pepper with a ream of blank white paper, but the moment something is printed on it, one doesn't think twice.*
– Georg Christoph Lichtenberg

*The blank white page contains the finest songs.* – Alphane Mallursset

There are those who set out from the blank white page and those rarer persons who end up there. Not without difficulty, for it sometimes takes a lot of scratching to recapture a bit of blank whiteness. Indeed, the sticky part is that being unsuited for writing does not suffice to remove the desire to write. In addition, a physiological deformity would be required. But even that wouldn't do it: certain individuals would find a way out by dictating.

In this domain, I personally have traveled a strange route whose circular nature is the mark of all the children of Bouvard and Pécuchet. Queneau went and figured out that the story of the two sow bugs (as Flaubert called them) was in fact, like many great European novels, an odyssey, a 'wandering about the Mediterranean of Knowledge.' My wandering took place on an infinitely more restricted Mediterranean, a minuscule sea of ink, on which float only, at the beginning as at the end of my voyage, a few sheets of blank white paper.

From early on, I had troubling relations with paper. It began when I was about eight and the oldest of my brothers took the happy initiative of bringing me to his office from time to time. I had a special fondness for these visits that gave me the impression of gaining access to a new world – that of adults, of business – from which most of my classmates were excluded in advance.

From the first of my visits, which took place on a bitterly cold day, I was particularly drawn first by the monumental typewriter, then by a tall, rather narrow set of roll-top shelves on which were stacked in neatly arranged piles various kinds of paper. Beautiful sheets of a nearly blinding whiteness that I imagined from what I could see to be light, fine, and crackly: some were completely virgin, others had a letterhead, and others still had a more mysterious appearance (no doubt various administrative forms). All their seductive power came from their not looking in any way like the grayish paper in my school notebooks. Not one single little square or the least hint of a horizontal line sullied their purity.

This profusion surprised me and increased still further the admiration I felt for this brother (who in any event never missed a chance to make me happy). Seeing me that day standing motionless before his stores of paper, he suggested that I help myself if I wanted to. For once I didn't need to be told something twice, and scarcely had he turned his back when, trembling with joy, I assembled a solid provision of paper, taking samples from each of the piles I managed to reach.

This was truly my first treasure. And since I had no place of my own in which to keep it, I put it just above my bed, behind the frame holding the portrait of my mother (which matched the frame mounted on the opposite wall holding the portrait of my father).

I had no idea what I might do with all this paper, for I was barely able to print in awkward, shaky, block letters on 'double-lined' paper the words and sentences that my teacher dictated to me (this was before I had become a good student).

Thinking carefully about it now, I wonder if I didn't have in mind the idea that one day I could turn this paper into money. At the time, we had only paper money: tiny little cardboard squares for the smallest sums – on the order of a few present-day centimes – bills of reduced size for slightly larger amounts (notes of a size and shape similar to those of the bills used in Italy when there was a shortage of one-hundred-lire coins). I had never had many of these bills at my disposal, and truth be told, I don't think I felt the need. But the idea of possessing, of having as my very own, the material that would allow me one day, if I so desired, to make them at will, undoubtedly must have seemed reassuring to me. In any event, it was in this form that there first appeared in me the desire for accumulation.

I must not have been satisfied with this first yet copious supply, for I made use of each of my subsequent visits to my brother as an opportunity to pretend I had immediate need of more and take a few additional sheets, which would then join the others that very night between the wall and painting, behind the smile and lightly pink cheeks of the portrait of my mother.

Later, as a high schooler, I gave special attention to the buying, always in quantities greater than was necessary, of appointment books, address books, registers, and ordinary notebooks, most of which were left untouched. The vast projects for which I destined them were already quite willing, even in those days, not to go beyond the project stage. And so, as the years went by, I found myself in command of a not insignificant collection of these precious auxiliaries whose cardboard covers were fading a bit and whose tightly quad-ruled pages were growing quite yellow with age, but which were nonetheless always ready to hold the expositions I intended for them and in fact already contained what was most essential. To the point that it would have seemed sacrilegious to carry out the slightest substitution among them, haunted as they all were by the sentences they should have been bearing for a long time.

A few years later, it was those large registers bound in black cloth (which one still finds in certain specialized stationery stores near the Bibliothèque Nationale) that I began accumulating with the same zeal as my childhood notebooks.

80

Finally, very recently I discovered, first in Venice, then in New York, exactly what I had so long been seeking: objects that look like books in every way except that they contain nary a printed word. The ones from Venice are, as they should be, remarkable above all for their choice paper and the quality of their binding, while the less prestige-conscious, more practical New York model has a white jacket on both sides of which is printed in bold, black letters – except for the o in *Nothing*, which is printed in fine, raised, bright red type – this somewhat provocative title: *The Nothing Book*. I don't know what sudden sense of propriety prevented me, in the one as in the other case, from buying more than two copies of these works so rich in potentialities. I probably didn't wish to overinflate the volume of my 'œuvre': fictitious as it was, it still had to be confined to plausible dimensions.

To this day I maintain a dual attitude toward paper. Standard quad-ruled French notebook paper I use only reluctantly: its little squares imprison me. Blank white paper impresses me, so I do everything I can to protect its purity. In this way, I have come to be interested with a kind of passion in the use others make of their paper and, when the occasion arises, cannot help taking a quick look at the drafts, notes, and manuscripts that come before my eyes (those belonging to my friends, of course, but also those belonging to strangers with whom I happen to come in contact in the places where I work). Not to decipher indiscreetly the contents, but simply to observe the relationship between what is written and what it is written on. Certain hands shock me for their lack of consideration. They greedily spread out over pages and pages, paying no mind to rulings, making a mockery of margins, spilling over all limits, and projecting their vigorous members in all possible directions. From a distance they seem to be a part of the paper itself, to have forever been embedded in it. Mine has no notion of these conqueror's ways. Never does it plunge violently into the great void provided by the sheet of paper offered to it. Respectfully, it lingers for a long time at the edge. It does not attack; it grazes, caresses with the tip of the pen, as if it had first to tame the savage page. And the process continues accordingly. When I have filled a page, it seems scarcely touched, and in the white space I maintain around my texts, another could easily fit his own.

I came quite naturally to privilege the short forms, precisely those that demand the least paper. I imagine ways of reducing a text the way one reduces a sauce. For me, an aphorism, provided it is well constructed, is an advantageous replacement for a philosophical elaboration. At times a simple sentence suffices where a page would be too much, but a sentence such that it echoes long and far.

## MOMENTARY PAUSE NUMBER TWO

*I*t is high time, reader, once again to give you the chance to speak. You
agreed without flinching to follow the author down the risky paths
of his past. You saw him born or reborn at the intersection of several
discomforts, several ambiguities. With him you have taken long strides
along the paths leading from stage to stage in a life short on events.
Stages that have one trait in common: they have all led him to the same
impasse.

'About time!' you are going to say. 'What is he waiting for to draw the
unavoidable conclusions? Since works are the only mirror that allows
the artist to see himself in his true dimension, our man should assuredly
not harbor any further illusions regarding his gifts as a maker of literature.
And anyway he has no call to be upset about it. He should just go ahead
and accept renouncing the world of telling and writing, and if he did, at
least he would be free of the obligation of telling and writing about how
he's renouncing the world.'

'Definitely! There's a most honorable way out that he will be most
grateful to you for having suggested.'

'Why doesn't he hurry up and take it?'

'Everything's pushing him that way, and yet I doubt he'll resign himself
to it.'

'Are you finally going to tell us why?'

'Quite simply, it's that he believes that one day he'll be able to make
something of his deficits.'

'What? Turn his failure into a work of art? Resort to the shameful trick
of making a book out of the debris of the ones he hasn't written? He who
admits having once dreamed so devotedly of a real masterpiece would
stoop to patching together scraps of work?'

'And why not? What does he have to lose? Whatever he does, he still has his childhood dream of the liberating book. This mirage never stops driving his gaze. But to be freed of it, looking elsewhere is not enough: his eye sees nothing in things save the absence of what he seeks. Is it not best for him to accept this state of affairs? And so he has decided to describe patiently the outlines of this absence, to sketch the forms with the most precision possible.'

'More power to him, but in that case he'd better remember this: it's one thing to want to turn your failure into a work of art and another to fuss over it as if it already were ...'

# HEROES

*Proposition: during a harsh winter, burn books.* – Georg Christoph Lichtenberg

*I do not know if it is necessary to go on writing. Fine minds have had their doubts. Marcel Schwob was not far from thinking, in the spirit of Renan, that the efforts of the classical and romantic generations left us only one domain to explore, that of the literature of erudition.* – Jean Paulhan

*Everything has been said – everything that is great and simple to say – over the course of the millennia during which mankind has pondered and squandered. Everything has been said that was profound in relation to the elevation of the point of view, that is to say both extensive and vast. Today one can only repeat . . . , only trivial details still remain unexplored . . . to mankind today there remains the most thankless and the least glamorous job, that of filling in the gaps with squirming little details.* – Pierre Reverdy

*We know, we feel that everything has been said, that there is nothing left to say. But we feel less that this truth affords language a strange, even unsettling status which redeems it. Words are ultimately saved because they have ceased living.* – E. M. Cioran

*Speaking frightens me because, never saying enough, I thus always say too much.* – Jacques Derrida

Decidedly there is no such thing as a 'good' practical joke. I had thought myself capable of making last indefinitely the little game of delicately balancing extended illusions and deferred deadlines that I had first set up as a child. After all, I was its only master, its only official, and I was beginning to know its ins and outs quite well.

In point of fact, I found myself trapped. My dreams of glory — still lovingly coddled, albeit with an ever greater discretion — had, without too much difficulty, survived the early disappointments. One day they left for good, slipping out on tiptoe, tired no doubt of having waited too long for their cue to enter. From then on the game appeared to me as it really is: absent of meaning, of purpose.

The ironic distance I imposed upon myself in relation to the commitments of my friends, who one after another found — with an ease that still disconcerts me — the group with which they would then long identify themselves (clan, party, family, or splinter group), gradually put me out of the running. In the end, my mistrust of fads and leaders and my desire to make my thought something other than the echo of the various rumblings that surrounded me simply tied my own hands. To the point of being nothing more, in matters intellectual, than a kind of ghostly wanderer, a man who wasn't a big wheel in any circle. And of these long years, which little by little began to run together in my memory, now forming something like a fused, or rather frozen, block, I recall only a solitary march toward I don't know what kind of writing, a slow, hesitant march delayed indefinitely by the intimate conviction, from time to time reaffirmed, that, in any event, writing is futile. I gauge the enormous power regret confers on things and dutifully concentrate on the roads I have not taken, on the initiatives I have preferred not to seize.

1

Telling my story, using my own experiences to illustrate the themes of exile, uprootedness, and cultural mixing – even though, in the eyes of many, these issues still passed for commonplaces whose raising was purely academic – would surely have allowed me, without much effort, to establish myself as an innovator. The undertaking was without risk. My situation was distinctive enough to offer a pinch of exoticism that would spice up the exposition in just the right places, and my life path was universal enough to allow anyone willing to make a few little changes to recognize himself in it. So many unexpected or amusing little aspects and in the end a childhood like all others.

But at that point I scorned the idea of describing my house with its wrought-iron doors, the long rooms opening one onto the next, and the fountain in its star-shaped basin in the middle of the garden, scorned the idea of using anecdotes to sketch the widely varying portraits of all the different members of my family. On the contrary, what I would have wanted was to lend a definitive existence – beyond any anecdote and by using a method I had yet to find – to that house and its inhabitants, to add an additional link to the chain of places and characters that serve as references for readers' imaginations. A task to which I of course did not feel equal. Besides, my feelings were still so ambiguous that I would not even have known what tint to give this evocation. Sometimes I remembered my Moroccan years as a paradise lost, sometimes as the time I had termed that of the 'anterior exile' or of 'bad exoticism.' Likewise, my moment of first settling alone in the dingy, gray Paris of the mid-1950s (which still reeked fully and thoroughly of the postwar) struck me alternately as the dreamed-of return to the Promised Land and as the occasion for a premature and painful alienation. Coming back to these ambiguities after so many years away would have meant openly admitting that a grieving process had not been completed, one that furthermore had never seriously been initiated.

Then, too, I could not help seeing as a worrisome symptom my starting with an autobiography. Gushing over my childhood was decidedly not a noble enough task. I would have wished first to take a long detour, to throw myself into a completely novel undertaking that went against my natural inclination and was as far removed as possible from what one could expect from me: a bold stroke about which I would have been proud later to laugh to my heart's content. Only then would I have won the right to lazily mine my memory.

Truth be told, when I had the courage to take my way of thinking to its logical conclusion, it was all forms of the literature of confession that it seemed necessary to avoid. I could sense only too well the risks of investigating the self. Once one starts down this slippery slope, bad faith becomes queen, and even the historian's much-flaunted scruples serve as mere window dressing for a histrionic display. A pitiful little scene, by the way, in which the person saying 'I' is always changing parts, as in a detective story whose author is both victim and criminal, both investigator and witness . . . and judge too, just for good measure! Thus, the whole business was full of traps and pitfalls that I endeavored to list with vengeful zeal without asking myself if a certain number of them were not, at the expense of a slight effort, avoidable.

So it is that still today I envy those whose lives have value as an example when narrated plainly. If they dream, their dreams are those of our society; if they are worried, their worries are those of our time. They have only to speak and everyone immediately recognizes himself or herself in them.

'Who,' I would ask myself, 'would ever think to recognize himself in me? The memories I am so careful to preserve are unusable. They go back to a world that few people knew and that is more or less dead now. Why resuscitate it? For whom? By leaving it, haven't I lost the right to speak in its name?'

The idea that others – hypothetical readers – could find my story interesting one day would have struck me as silly. Did not they themselves have their own memories? Were they not also stuck in their own ruts? How would I manage to overcome their repulsion with my words? What means of breaking down doors would I have had to use simply to overcome their (perfectly justified) indifference, let alone their resistance? A single example was enough for me: would I ever succeed in evoking for someone who knows nothing of Hebrew its sonorities and rhythms, the kind of musical pleasure (and all but sensual one as well, despite the supposed austerity of such moments) brought me by prayers at High Holidays in the beginning of the fall, prayers at once more tuneful and more laden with ceremony than the songs sung on ordinary Saturdays?

I quickly convinced myself that it is fruitless to write so long as one has no idea of one's audience, so long as one has met no one to whose demands one can reply, in whose encouragement one can believe, in whose judgment one can take pride. Lacking these supports and therefore ill-equipped to fulfill one of its basic functions – being a source at least of a form of recognition – the story of my life would have been good for nothing. Out of pasts exalted and magnified at will, others have been able to create epics that evidence a judicious marriage of a bit of memory with much fantasy. I managed to make this only into another hindrance.

I didn't have to protect myself so carefully from the dangers of the diary – a kind of reasoned repulsion had preserved me from it, and I could not imagine conceding the smallest scrap of space to this chancre that would have made short work of destroying everything. The absence of any constraint, of any form, of any rule, would have led me to the very place I did not want to go: the lukewarm desert of narcissism and self-indulgence. Amiel had taught me a few of the ridiculous traits that cling to such an exercise: the overinflated details, the numerous bits of trivia, and especially the progressive acceptance of inactivity (which, to top it all off, one thinks one is fighting through childish exhortations one addresses to oneself). I was burdened enough by my own shortcomings to be careful not to bring in new ones. For I knew full well that once the starting gun had been fired, I would not be able to resist the temptation of making too much of it and would constantly be trying to seduce or shock, to win the complicity of a reader who by definition didn't exist. No, clearly, it was something not to be taken up, something that, at best, looked to me like a never-ending makeup review session for the entrance exam to the writers' club.

## 2

I clearly saw one solution: it would have been enough for me to turn resolutely toward fiction, to dare throw myself into the imaginary, to hack through all the knots with great blows from my saber, to invent heroes who would unfetter me, and finally to construct, through a combination of patience and skill, a mythic figure who would have made me tolerable to myself. But there too, things, as usual, proved less simple than they first seemed.

As one might have expected, from the time I began reading, I had identified with all kinds of characters whom I combined as my fancy saw fit (Ulysses and Robinson Crusoe, Jonah and Gulliver, Hercules and Samson, Job and Don Quixote), which permitted me to journey continually among several universes. But a new and important step was taken when I happened to discover (while flipping as usual through the books of one of my brothers) the resources and treasures of allegorical interpretation. It was a kind of bedazzlement. So the adventures of the heroes in my tattered *Tales and Legends* volumes were not gratuitous! They had a meaning. Better still, they spoke to me about myself, and about nothing else. One taught me insolence and disrespect, and I promised myself not to forget the lesson (which I nonetheless hurried to do); another showed me how multiplicity of form could serve to protect identity. I reviewed these fabulous ancestors and from then on was not astonished to find them so close. Sisyphus, Penelope, Tantalus, even the pale Danaides: like me, they were all victims of the impossibility of bringing to an end the task assigned them, yet possessed with the desire always to start over.

But as time went by, the object of my spontaneous identifications evolved and grew more precise even as it migrated toward completely different horizons. I began finding resemblances between myself and all antiheroes real or imaginary: the gentle, debased dreamers of the ghettos; honest people who found themselves persecuted; the pure of heart victimized by their purity; the ones against the world; unrecognized geniuses – in short, all the five-footed sheep treated like scabby beasts, all the eagles taken by the shortsighted people around them for lame ducks. I cherished them, and their ultimate triumphs were of course my triumphs. All the same, at times it would happen that I would feel hesitant with regard to certain reversals of fortune. When the final revelation took place, when the unrecognized decent man ended up winning everyone's appreciation, I was not always satisfied. In these miraculous resolutions I smelled too strong an odor of a simple bit of trickery on the part of the author without any necessary relation to what might have been the truth. I suddenly discovered that I didn't like this enchanted universe where it was enough to say things for them to be taken as true.

I was in no hurry to enter the world of the imaginary for my own account – there was too much freedom there and a form of power that I feared abusing in advance. For fiction too has its dangers. More perfidiously than confession pure and simple, it strips. What to do so as not to fall into the nets of those who profess to analyze? I lavished learned instructions upon myself: 'When you decide to show around a few of your pages,' I said to myself, 'remember that they no longer belong to you. Your readers will look not only for what you have tried to say, but also for what you have tried to hide from their gaze. They will know how to be more insightful than you will have been sly and will see your ruses, your disguises, your mysteries. The worst, however, is not that they will end up stripping you naked, the worst is that for your barely glimpsed image they are more than likely to substitute whatever mirage might happen to satisfy them at that particular moment.' And, reflecting on the rivers of inept nonsense I had seen rush over several authors near and dear to me, I dreaded having to fall one day into the hands of certain of those adepts who, armed with their poorly sharpened scalpels and their rusty bars, judge themselves capable of discerning a cry beneath a silence, a sign behind such and such an absence, and in denial itself the traces of a confession.

So then I dreamed of strictly guarded anonymity, of a subtle game of pseudonyms that would put the sharpest of those blood-hounds off the trail. I even began perfecting a whole battery of imaginary identities of which precious few to this point – is it necessary to say it? – have found an occasion to be used. My method was the simplest kind imaginable: I conceived of each of these names not as a mask but as a kind of experimental me that, in the manner of an originally gracelessly proportioned face to which surgery has succeeded in bringing a bit of harmony, would pin down a few coherent traits of mine of a sort likely to give the reader the illusion of dealing with an original figure. I would have had all these pseudonyms float around in the world like so many trial balloons while I, invisible, observed their behavior. I even told myself that in fact nothing in the end prevented my identifying

93

for real with the one that had succeeded the most completely. Thus, on the pretext of protecting my identity and in hopes of giving free rein to a few of my possible facets, I was completely ready, if not to repudiate the last name my father gave me – as heavy to bear some days as a hobbled caribou – then at least to dissociate it radically from my works to come.

At bottom, all my trouble came from having stuck with the ideology I had in my twenties, which viewed literature only as revelation. I had not yet understood what is no doubt taught to children in today's schools, to wit, that a book need not be the reflection or transcription of something that exists before it; it simply is. Thus, one can create it out of whole cloth, without fear or restraint, since it has no other justification than in and of itself. To skirt the obstacles that had obstructed me until then, I would have had to find a way of writing that risks neither sidetracking nor spotlighting its author. A kind of writing, in other words, that would be self-generating.

I have looked for it everywhere.

# LACUNA

*The thought that escaped was what I wished to write; I write instead that it has escaped me.* – Blaise Pascal

Here the author must confess his great embarrassment to the reader. The notes that were to be used in drafting this chapter have disappeared, and alas, he no longer has either the time to look for them or the strength to reconstruct them. The indulgent reader should thus be kind enough to note that in the original outline, this chapter was in fact devoted to a long conversation (or rather a debate, really) with the reader.

The author planned finally to justify his approach, an approach that led him to deliver a text that is continually being weighted down with its own commentaries. Indeed, who knows whether the reader appreciates the constant interventions interrupting his or her reading to correct and reshape the ongoing exposition? Does this need to add nuances – ones which are, of course, useful, nay indispensable, at times, but which at others are so tenuous that they could easily, in the work of a less scrupulous author (of which there are many, particularly in our day and age), be omitted without this omission's damaging for all that the balance of the work as a whole, quite the contrary – this mania for tempering (almost) every assertion with a bit of mockery (which seemingly allows one to speak without too much embarrassment about the most embarrassing things), this haste in the end to defuse each admission with a bit of sarcasm (as if it hadn't long been known that making fun of oneself is only a way of taking oneself seriously slightly less crude than others), not all risk resulting, at the end of the road, in the dislocation – harmful in more than one sense – of an original utterance that was already rather lacking in clarity?

To these observations, made without any real nastiness by the reader, the author responded with a passionate argument, a veritable piece of grand oratory in the style of the ancients.

97

He was well aware, he said, of all these weaknesses. But to his way of thinking, this text was not a solid block and should in no way be taken as such. He had never claimed to have produced a rigorous discourse devoid of flaws. He himself was not (something, truth be told, he knew only too well) one of those glorious colossi whose agile logos – into which glide with unequaled grace (and as if part of a veritable gala) multitudinous glosses – lose the reader in their glad gallopings all the more elegantly to trammel him.

Furthermore, he did not claim that his irony (or mockery) was entirely innocent. But at least it suggested an angle of approach and informed those who might not spontaneously have located it that a general line was at work here. As for the rest, he was prepared to acknowledge that nothing of what he had said was truly original: more than one passage had even struck him upon rereading as being roughly as new as an annually recycled almanac pun. But what of it? If one wanted certain truths to be able to go on living, did they not have to be said over and over again? After all, things remain in existence only thanks to the effort made by a few people to recreate them day after day.

And to finish, he went on to say, what he wished to do was raise a bit of anxiety, provoke a bit of uneasiness – if mild, if fleeting – in those who, to this point, gave themselves over in all tranquility to literary activity, and on the other hand to return a bit of calm to all those who suffered from not being able to write.

This succinct summary of that passionate debate should at least permit the reader to tackle the reading of the next chapter without any handicap.

## LAST WORD

*... A book that is an architectural, premeditated book, and not a collection of random inspirations, marvelous though they might be.* – Stéphane Mallarmé

*Why can a book not live up to the necessity of writing it?* – J. Vicens

Here there has come practically to its end this which bears a strong resemblance to a book: the result in any event of an accumulation of chapters grouped around a theme. If I dare say it, these pages were written without any of the difficulties, without (almost) any of the obstacles that they are forever denouncing. It will be understood, then, why I am again taking up what was asserted (but, as one may recall, not justified) from the first chapter: *ceci n'est pas un livre*. For, it is easy to realize, the object that you, reader, currently have in hand is in no way comparable to the one for which I have so long borne desire within me, without completely resigning myself to mourning it. That desired object was adorned with splendor and solemnity and intimately linked to a thousand hopes. It is thus only just to my way of thinking that, for the sake of the very safety of the language, one and the same word should not designate two such heterogeneous realities. Unless it is to admit that – source of infinite complications – we are speaking here of a (regrettable) case of homonymy.

But since the reader has been willing to follow me while I glossed imaginary books, he will perhaps forgive my also offering him a few explanations regarding the origins of this (quite real) nonbook.

1

Accordingly, from then on I accepted a book's function as being not a useless redoubling of reality but its continuation by other means. The only thing I had to do was find said means, and fast.

The best, of course, was to turn against literature those weapons – unknown to many but formidable – that, in experienced hands, are the very ambiguities and weaknesses of language. I decided that my effort would aim above all to employ my own user's ruses against the pitfalls of writing (or rather, against its pitiful annoyances): from now on it would be lure for lure, ploy for ploy. Perhaps it would cease to be an unfair fight.

Braving the most venerable prohibitions, even positing this transgression as method, I tried my hand at all the blasphemies, at all the sacrileges, mixing – as had all those who had preceded me down this path that was much more beaten than I had imagined – extreme childishness with extreme seriousness. Provisionally disburdened of my vast projects, I relearned the rudiments of the craft, approaching writing at its most elemental levels: the letter and the syllable, the cipher and even the mere punctuation mark. Having started from there, I no longer hesitated to declare all borders erased: between words, between sentences, between pages, between works. Thus there began to appear to me in the heart of the most familiar texts blank spaces, gaps, missing parts, true voids in fact that suddenly were proliferating. I hastened to plaster them over with opaque words obtained in abundance through a whole host of reroutings.

Thus I discovered that if one is the least bit welcoming in one's treatment of it, a word never comes alone. It brings along with it all those that belong to its clan – its kin by virtue of sense or sound – which quite obviously were awaiting only that breach created by one of their gang to come bursting forth. I let them do as they pleased, or better still, urged them forward, blazing the trail for them in a thousand ways. And with the merest waving of my pen, I made Hugo the humblest of men, a worn-down chap out hawking hackneyed lines, a cellar whence to fetch them like cheap wines. And even Racine, that thoroughbred of the subtle weaving of sinuosities, I used as a rhyme morgue. I liked to set out in search of Edgar Allan Poe's bed and reveal that it could be located only in his reading room. With the complicity of an expert peer who soon became a master (for he could pare exquisite meaning from seemingly idle play), I succeeded on certain days in making emerge from within a country priest's house – deliciously dated yet still endowed with all its former graces amid a brilliant enclosure of vegetation – a solid troop of workers walking, jostling each other good-naturedly, and even in seeing henceforth on a famous page in the white letters only the white's letter.

Opposing the most sacred injunctions, I sought new ways to flout syntax, finding sense in the most disjointed of utterances and the most incoherent of sequences. I grew accustomed to leading the simplest phrases and idioms surreptitiously away from their current accepted meanings into new ones better suited to my needs. I particularly liked using words that ordinarily only have meaning if one has taken care to imprison them behind the double wall of quotation marks.

In the manner of Queneau drawing the material for *The Bark Tree* from *Discourse on Method*, I set out to turn a treatise on rhetoric into an adventure story and a very well known anthology for students into a love story. I even wanted to broaden the experiment to take in other categories of books: dictionaries, encyclopædias, chronologies, even (after all, why not?) the white and yellow pages. I reproached myself from time to time for liking pastiche overmuch: why insist on reproducing dead forms indefinitely? 'But,' I would tell myself over and over, 'is one ever sure that a form is really dead before having killed it a little oneself?'

Gripped suddenly by the euphoria characteristic of convalescents, I had the impression of being able to fly. I had finished with apathy, drowsiness, indolence, inertia, languor, listlessness, numbness, torpor. I was as if consumed by flame: a flame that had been a long time kindling but that I fervently hoped would be every bit as long in going out. I rid myself in one fell swoop of the symmetric naivetés of lyricism and cynicism. I no longer even felt obliged, when getting a laugh, to laugh at myself first.

103

Having made up my mind to take nothing seriously but derision, I sincerely believed that I had only to be published to appear in public letters as an exceptional being.

Chance and friendship did the rest.

## 2

A nd so I put to myself a question that struck me as unusual and set out in search of a few possible answers. At first I thought there would be nothing interesting to be found in this pursuit (which is why I was so slow to embark upon it). The diagnosis was so easy: an all but classic case of indolence, of running away from creative effort, of lacking aptitude for taking one's desire seriously. One can give all this any number of more or less disparaging names, the least perhaps being the one Flaubert almost kept as the title of *Sentimental Education*: withered fruit. My word, I was assuredly neither the first nor the last of these scarcely completed products from a puny plant.

As I first conceived it, this work would thus in fact have been a kind of token: the interminable paraphrase of a few elementary propositions none of which would have held my attention for an instant had I been obliged to be the reader.

And then I realized that maybe there was something else, and I suddenly understood this obvious fact (which apparently had escaped me until then): there is an infinite distance between the individual act of writing and the social fact of creating books. Now with me, for years the essence of my work had consisted of making thorough use of writing not to make literature but to put off its production. Dancing around words and ceaselessly challenging everything whose mission it is to provide security was all I ever did. Under such circumstances, how could I have managed to cover the distance separating me from the book?

I could have placed myself under the patronage of Artaud and found a justification for my undertaking in the liminal declaration of *Umbilical Limbo*: 'There where others offer works, I claim to do no more than display my mind.' But my wish was more to find a form that would permit me to integrate the disparate multitude of fragments on one theme amassed over the years and, after having subjected them to an intense distillation, to draw a few pages from the process that I hoped would be strong. At the same time, I wanted to end up with a work such that at any moment one would have the impression that anything is still possible, a work in which the meaning would not come from some authorial decree but would be the fruit of an internal progression (whose ultimately being completable one day nothing guarantees).

An answer finally emerges.

Giving shape to the very thing that is the principal object of my fear (to write or not to write) — could that be the way to escape (however little) from the vicious circle of stupor and paralysis? A step perhaps toward a minor form of mastery? Proust himself seems obsessed by the idea that he will never be able to write 'his book,' and it is by dint of repeating this fear that he moves forward in his own story.

Thus, writing that one would like to write is already writing. Writing that one cannot write is still writing. One way as good as another of accomplishing the reversal that is at the origin of so many audacious undertakings: making of the peripheral the central, of the incidental the essential, of the scrap rock the cornerstone. So I knew what was left to me to do: a kind of tour de force by which I would have to manage to give fictive existence to books that don't really exist, thereby giving real existence to the book that deals with those fictitious books. A move in short that bears a strong resemblance to the one leading up to the Cartesian *cogito*. It was to be part of the very moment when I would formally acknowledge my inaptitude for writing that I would discover myself to be a writer, and it was to be the absence of my uncompleted works on which this one would feed. A fine example of the loser-wins strategy, of that bit of dialectic sleight of hand that makes of a collection of failures a path toward success. How often we've been told that Sisyphus built muscles!

## FAREWELL TO THE READER

This cadence looks weak to you, reader? But who knows how one should have concluded? Like you, the author is not unaware that in terms of importance, the last lines are in no way inferior to the first ones. But what's the good of increasing the number of final words? All the tricks in the world won't give a definitive conclusion to these pages, which are not capable of having one.

'Oh, one more push!' you say. 'Just a little more effort and we'll let you go.'

Well, let's say that in the final analysis, this text could claim to be a very classic novel. Is it not the story of an ever deferred meeting, of a frustrated love strewn with obstacles and crosspieces which is the victim of illusions and regrets? Of an unhappy and perhaps ultimately impossible love, that of its author for a certain idea of literature.

*In truth I know not what must be won-*
*dered at more: the great goodness of the*
*men who welcome such poor essays, or*
*my incredible confidence in casting such*
*foolishnesses into the world.* – Maurice
de Guérin, *The Green Notebook*

# THE AUTHOR

Marcel Bénabou, born in Meknès (Morocco) on 29 June 1939.

A professor of ancient history at the University of Paris VII, he has published a book entitled *La résistance africaine à la romanisation* (African resistance to romanization), F. Maspero, 1976, as well as various articles on Roman history.

The definitively provisional secretary of Oulipo, he is also the author of

*Voies de vieux temps* (Old-time ways), L'Inattendu, 1976.

*Un aphorisme peut en cacher un autre* (One aphorism can hide another), Bibliothèque Oulipienne, no. 13.

*Locutions introuvables* (Impossible-to-find expressions), Bibliothèque Oulipienne, no. 25.

*Alexandre au greffoir* (Alexander with the grafting tool), Bibliothèque Oulipienne, no. 29.

*Bris de mots* (Broken words), Bibliothèque Oulipienne, no. 40.

*La littérature potentielle* (Potential literature), (in collaboration), Gallimard, 1973.

All the above are available in *La Bibliothèque Oulipienne* (The Oulipian library), Seghers, 1990.

*Atlas de littérature potentielle* (Atlas of potential literature), (in collaboration), Gallimard, 1981.

*Presbytère et prolétaires: Le dossier PALF* (Presbytery and proletarians: The automatic production of French literature file), (in collaboration with Georges Perec), Limon, 1989. Also published as *Cahiers Georges Perec* 3.

*Jette ce livre avant qu'il soit trop tard* (Throw this book away before it's too late), Seghers, 1992.

*Jacob, Ménahem et Mimoun: Une epopée familiale* (Jacob, Menachem, and Mimoun: a family epic), Editions du Seuil, 1995.